# LEBRON JAMES

## THE MAKING OF AN MVP

**TERRY PLUTO** and **BRIAN WINDHORST**
with photographs from The Plain Dealer

**Gray & Company, Publishers**
Cleveland

# Dedication

*To Jim Muth, the Benedictine teacher who made me believe I could be a writer.* — TERRY PLUTO

*To the family, friends and doctors who helped me through the summer of 2008.* — BRIAN WINDHORST

© 2009 by Terry Pluto and Brian Windhorst
Photographs © *The Plain Dealer*,
except where otherwise credited

 Gray & Company, Publishers
Cleveland, Ohio
www.grayco.com

Book and cover design by David Kordalski
Picture editing by Bill Gugliotta
Typefaces: Stag, Scout, Miller

Library of Congress Cataloging-in-Publication Data

Pluto, Terry
LeBron James: The Making of an MVP / Terry Pluto and Brian Windhorst.
p. cm.

ISBN 978-1-59851-059-1

1. James, LeBron. 2. Basketball players -- United States -- Biography. 3. Cleveland Cavaliers
(Basketball team) -- History. I. Windhorst, Brian. II. Title.

GV884.J36P59 2009
796.323092--dc22
[B]
2009041865

Printed in the United States of America
10 9 8 7 6 5 4 3 2

PLAIN DEALER PHOTOGRAPHS | JOHN KUNTZ, ABOVE; TRACY BOULIAN, TITLE PAGE

# Contents.

PLAIN DEALER PHOTOGRAPH | TRACY BOULIAN

## MVP SEASON MOMENTS

Heaving chalk into the air while letting out a deep breath has become a LeBron James trademark.

PLAIN DEALER PHOTOGRAPHS | JOHN KUNTZ; TRACY BOULIAN

**LeBron accepted his MVP Award in one of his favorite places, St. Vincent-St. Mary High School.**

PLAIN DEALER PHOTOGRAPH | GUS CHAN

# Chapter 1. The Ceremony

LeBron James could have held the ceremony anywhere. How about Quicken Loans Arena, where 20,562 fans stand and stomp and scream at the mere mention of his name when the starting lineup is introduced for the Cleveland Cavaliers? Or how about the fanciest club in downtown Cleveland? Maybe the Oregon-based headquarters of his biggest sponsor. Or even Beverly Hills, if he wanted some Hollywood flavor on the West Coast. The National Basketball Association would have loved LeBron to go to New York for the award, transforming it into an event for NBA TV and every other national network. After all, the 24-year-old was about to receive what many believed would be his first of several Most Valuable Player awards.

*MVP…MVP…MVP…*

Night after night throughout the 2008-09 season, that chant rocked Quicken Loans Arena as the Cavaliers racked up a 39-2 record on their home court.

*MVP…MVP…MVP…*

One spring afternoon, that battle cry echoed all over the Palace of Auburn Hills as the visiting Cavaliers were sweeping the Detroit Pistons out of the first round of the 2009 playoffs. It was the same court where LeBron and the Cavs were rudely booted out of the playoffs in Game 7 of the 2006 Eastern Conference Finals — only this time, there were as many Cavaliers fans in the house as Pistons fans watching the decline of their once-proud team.

*MVP…MVP…MVP…*

Now, those three letters were being screamed by high school kids from St. Vincent-St. Mary, the inner-city parochial school off West Market Street in the shadow of downtown Akron, Ohio. That's because in the spring of 2009 LeBron James chose to come here — home — for the ceremony at which

he would receive the National Basketball Association's Most Valuable Player award.

He walked into the gym, built in 1950, with cement block walls painted white and green, where the side baskets have old, square, wooden backboards and the seats are long, wooden bleachers.

*MVP…MVP…MVP…*

LeBron James stepped to the podium, in a dark blue business suit with a light blue tie, looking as much like a young corporate executive as the 24-year-old star of the Cleveland Cavaliers. He only revealed his nerves by bouncing his fingers a bit on the podium. He took a deep breath and stared at the packed gym where he'd starred for the St. Vincent-St. Mary Fighting Irish when they were the nation's top-ranked high school team in 2003.

LeBron was here to talk about winning the NBA MVP award, which he had done in a landslide with 109 out of a possible 121 first-place votes.

He thanked his teammates, coaches, friends and family.

He also thanked great players such as Oscar

Robertson, Magic Johnson, Kareem Abdul-Jabbar and Julius Erving "who laid this path before me."

That displayed an awareness rare among the young stars of the NBA. LeBron knows that the basketball galaxy did not begin with Michael Jordan. During his rookie year, LeBron was thrilled to meet Oscar Robertson, and knew the Hall of Fame guard once averaged a triple-double for a season when he was a star with the old Cincinnati Royals in the 1960s. He is truly touched to be mentioned in the same paragraph with any of the greats. By mentioning them in his address to an audience of teenagers, he did more than give a quick nod to history. He stressed that history mattered, that carrying on the legacy of the great players who came before him was part of being an MVP.

"When it comes to LeBron, the 'P' in the MVP award should also stand for 'Person,'" Cavaliers owner Dan Gilbert has often said.

There is a part of LeBron James's personality that makes him want to please, to be a good person, to make his family, friends and hometown proud — which is why he came to Akron for the MVP award. He stood at the podium in the gym and waited for the MVP chants to quiet down. When he spoke he was composed, clear and, in his own way (even without notes), prepared.

"I graduated from here six years ago," said LeBron. "I'm not that far away from this school ... it has helped me become the man I am today."

Is LeBron James an MVP?

No doubt.

You can recite the numbers: an average of 28.4 points per game, 7.6 assists, 7.2 rebounds and finishing second to Orlando center Dwight Howard in the voting for the NBA's 2009 Defensive Player of the Year.

"To be 24 years old and accepting this award, I never thought it would happen this fast," said LeBron, looking at the students and teachers in the bleachers through eyes fighting back a couple of tears.

**THE LEBRON FILE**
LeBron shares a birthday, December 30, with Tiger Woods. Both have endorsement deals with Nike, but they didn't meet until 2008, at an Orlando Magic game, where Woods is a season ticket holder.

"LeBron could have accepted the award in Cleveland," said Patty Burdon, a James family friend who does public relations work for the school. "I bet the NBA would have preferred to have this at the Q [Quicken Loans Arena], but LeBron's office called and said he wanted to do it here — at home."

LeBron told Burdon that he wanted only the teachers and students to be admitted.

He arrived at the school in a $200,000 gray Ferrari with the top down and vanity license plates reading "WITNESS". Waiting for him outside the school were fans and students, along with television crews, all lining the streets. Police were there to keep order.

It was so different from when he first came to St. Vincent-St. Mary at the age of 14 in 1999. He was a young man who grew up in a mostly black, inner-city Akron environment and now was attending a mostly white, rather upscale private school where nearly every student would attend college and teachers had little patience for fools or slackers in the classroom.

A story seldom told is how LeBron graduated with a "B" average. How he was on the honor roll during his senior year. How he was only in trouble a few times for "yelling in the hallway," according to Headmaster David Rathz. LeBron could stand proudly in front of those students not only because he's the greatest high school player ever to come out of Northeast Ohio, or because he could now put the initials MVP next his name. He was a real student athlete, one who was recruited by universities such as Duke, North Carolina and Stanford. In his junior year it became clear that there would be no college, that LeBron was headed to the NBA. But he had earned the grades to attend those schools, if that had been his plan.

On his way to the high school for the MVP ceremony, LeBron got off Interstate 77 at a different exit from the one he normally took.

"I took the long route," he told the students. "I went on some of those old roads that I used to walk. To ride on those roads you grew up on brought back some memories."

LeBron lived in about 10 different places while growing up — including two critical years with Pam and Frankie Walker, who gave him stability. He talked about having big dreams, but how people from Akron were not supposed to be able to dream big.

"When we were 11 years old, LeBron said he was going to turn pro after a year of college," said Sian (SEE-ahn) Cotton, who played with LeBron in summer leagues and later at St. Vincent-St. Mary. "He first dunked in the seventh grade. We were in an AAU tournament in Cleveland at a place called the Hilltopper. We had been telling him for a while that he was too scared to dunk, he'd get up over the rim — then just lay it in. But that day, he got up really high and looked down and ... boom. He threw it down."

LeBron held the ceremony up for about 20 minutes because his mother, Gloria, was stuck in traffic. She was 16 when LeBron was born, and he is her only child. LeBron looked in her direction and said, "I don't know how you did it. I'm still trying to figure it out. I may be able to figure out how to dunk a basketball or make a jumper, but I can't figure out how you raised me yourself."

*MVP...MVP...MVP...*

LeBron knew that many people had helped him win that award, and he wanted to mention them all.

The students wore T-shirts reading "WITNESS MVP." Rathz said the school was so proud that LeBron considered it home. "We don't want him to do anything for us, just keep coming back and saying hello like he's done. He does a great job of making people here feel good about what they did for him."

After winning the 2008 Olympic gold medal, he brought it to the school on Maple Street to show the teachers and some students. He comes to the school in private, not wanting the media or anyone outside of the Irish family to know he's there.

LeBron wanted someone else besides his family, friends and former summer league and high school coaches to join what he considers his second family at St. Vincent-St. Mary. He invited his Cavaliers teammates and coaches, and they all showed up.

"Individual accolades come when a team has success," LeBron said. "You look at those 14 guys over there — I got the award because of them. They put in the work."

Those Cavaliers indeed worked hard, but no harder than LeBron.

As Cavaliers General Manager Danny Ferry said when it was his turn to speak at the ceremony, "It takes a lot of sweat, and I'm sure he did a lot of sweating right here [in the high school gym]. I've been fortunate to watch him sweat [at the Cavs practice facility] when no one else was around. I just want to acknowledge that and give it a round of applause."

*MVP...MVP...MVP...*

Once again, the chant bubbled up from the students in the bleachers.

"I never dreamed about being MVP, but I'd be lying if I said I didn't enjoy this award," LeBron said. "Hard work does pay off. Dreams do come true ... This is the place where all my dreams started, where I thought they could become real. There really isn't a better place."

As part of the award, LeBron also received an automobile, a Kia Borrego SUV, which he donated to the Akron Urban League.

"LeBron never forgot where he came from," said Gloria James.

On that Monday afternoon, May 4, 2009, LeBron had the MVP trophy in his hands and maybe a tear or two in his eyes, and he didn't care if anyone thought it was corny or sentimental. To him, this was real life.

**NEXT PAGE: LeBron promised himself he wouldn't cry, but seeing his mother and friends in the crowd caused the new MVP to choke up.**

---

**THE 2009 MVP VOTING**

The top five vote getters for the 2008-09 season:

- LeBron James, Cleveland Cavaliers, 1,172 points
- Kobe Bryant, Los Angeles Lakers, 698 points
- Dwyane Wade, Miami Heat, 680 points
- Dwight Howard, Orlando Magic, 328 points
- Chris Paul, New Orleans Hornets, 192 points

---

# Chapter 2. Fitting In

During the 2009 MVP ceremony in the St. Vincent-St. Mary gym, LeBron looked out into the crowd and said, "Pam and Frankie Walker were instrumental in me being here and getting this award."

When people talk about those who helped shape LeBron James into a Most Valuable Player, you hear many names: his mother, Gloria; youth basketball coaches Dru Joyce II and Keith Dambrot; several pro coaches; NBA stars such as Kobe Bryant and Jason Kidd, who were LeBron's teammates on the 2008 Olympic team ...

But you seldom hear about the Walker family.

The Walkers met LeBron when he was a long-pencil-legged, sometimes scared, often shy 8-year-old. They remember him as a quiet, tall, skinny kid, a star on the peewee football field who scored 18 touchdowns in six games for the South Side Rangers coached by Frank Walker. They remember LeBron as a kid who needed some stability while his single mom went through a difficult time and they offered to take him in.

Gloria James was 16 when her son was born on December 30, 1984. She lived with her mother, Freda, who was known in her neighborhood as a giving woman, an excellent hairstylist and an anchor to her daughter, who now was a single mom. They lived in a large house on Hickory Street in Akron. But on Christmas Day, 1987, a week before LeBron's third birthday, Freda James died of a heart attack. Gloria was 19, on her own and unable to make enough money for her and her only child to stay in the house. LeBron has said in interviews

**By age 16, LeBron was already a star, but he had also endured significant personal hardships.**

that he moved about 10 times by his eighth birthday. Most times the new house or apartment was worse than the last place they stayed. Gloria sometimes seemed overwhelmed by the responsibility of being a mother on her own at such a young age.

When LeBron was in the fourth grade, the family moved several times and he was enrolled in different schools. In interviews, he has said he missed between 80 and 100 days of school. He stayed up late, watching television with Gloria. There was no stability, no strong male influence, no sense of structure in his life — except when LeBron played for the South Side Rangers. The Walker family and LeBron himself are very careful when they discuss this chaotic time of his life. They don't want it to reflect poorly on Gloria. At his MVP ceremony, LeBron stood in front of the crowd, looked at his mother, and said, "I still don't know how you did it." He meant how she managed to hold herself and LeBron together, despite all the challenges faced by a teenage single mother.

"Most people know LeBron as a superstar," said Pam Walker. "A while ago, my daughter said

PLAIN DEALER PHOTOGRAPH | MARVIN FONG

## MVP SEASON MOMENTS

LeBron has more dunks than any player in Cavaliers' team history.

PLAIN DEALER PHOTOGRAPH | JOSHUA GUNTER

that — 'Hey, LeBron is a superstar!'" Pam Walker laughed as she said that.

That's because they knew LeBron long before he became The Chosen One, a 17-year-old on the cover of Sports Illustrated, the first pick in the 2003 NBA draft. They knew him simply as a young boy who was well-mannered, athletically gifted and at a stage in his life when he was vulnerable to being pulled in the wrong direction.

When the Walker family agreed to take in LeBron, it was not to take him away from Gloria. It was simply to give him a place to stay, a family to help him feel secure. They had no clue that the NBA was in his future; they just wanted to help him avoid a future that included drugs, jail or other destruction that ravaged inner-city boys and men. The Walkers told Gloria that they believed in her, that she could visit her son at any time — that the arrangement was temporary, allowing her time to save some money and find a decent place to stay.

The identity of LeBron's biological father is not known, at least not publicly. A few men have made that claim, including one man who served some serious time in the Ohio prison system. But none produced any proof. Speculation in Akron has long been that the dad may have been Roland Bivins, who played basketball at Akron Central-Hower and was killed not long after high school. LeBron has never identified his biological father, and he does not welcome any questions about the subject. A close friend of Gloria's, Eddie Jackson, later came to be called "a father figure" by LeBron. He would help Gloria and LeBron during LeBron's high school years, and would be a key player in the early days of LeBron's negotiations with shoe companies. But Jackson never claimed to be LeBron's biological father, and he wasn't always there during LeBron's childhood.

LeBron needed stability. He needed a family.

To be an MVP, you need discipline. You need to understand that you are a part of a team. You need to respect authority. You can't always worry that someone else may be getting a more lucrative deal or better treatment. You need to know that being an MVP may mean you are the Most Valuable Player to the team, but you are not the only player.

It was with the Walker family that LeBron saw this modeled.

"I didn't know how he'd be when he moved in with us," said Pam Walker. "We had never brought anyone into our home before."

Would LeBron be angry because he wasn't with his mother? Would be rebel against authority, especially male authority? He'd never had any male authority figures in the home at this stage of his life. The Walkers also had two girls and a boy. Would LeBron battle with the other children? They had no legal authority over LeBron. They also didn't know how Gloria would react to them taking in her son.

The Walkers were a highly respected family. Frank Walker worked for the Akron Housing Authority (and later for the Akron Urban League). Pam Walker was an aide to Democratic congressman Tom Sawyer. (Later she worked for congressman Sherrod Brown and, when he moved up to the U.S. Senate, for Betty Sutton, who took his seat in the U.S. House of Representatives.) Gloria James had held mostly low-paying service jobs; at the Walkers, LeBron now saw people with true careers, and who expected the same from their children. He was around people who assumed college was in the future for their children, and who had friends with good jobs and college degrees. He was being exposed to a new world.

The Walkers talk about how polite LeBron was when he came to them, how he already had a personality that "likes to please" — traits he must have learned from his mother and grandmother. But he needed more. "We thought LeBron needed a routine," said Pam Walker. He learned to do homework after school. He learned to do chores such as dusting and washing dishes. He learned to get ready for school quickly because the Walkers already had three of their own children, so

that made six in a house with one bathroom. He learned to get up by 6:30 a.m. He learned that if he didn't wash up the night before, he'd be awakened even earlier the next morning so he would use the bathroom before everyone else.

The Walkers say LeBron embraced their style of living.

"What made it easy is that he loved it," said Pam Walker. "He really didn't fight us at all. He roomed with my son, Frankie, and it was Frankie who was being told to clean up his room. LeBron kept his side neat."

"They put the discipline act into me," said LeBron. "They made me get up every day and go to school. There were days I didn't want to go to school. Being part of a family, a mom-and-dad surrounding ... you had a brother and you had two sisters ... it was an unbelievable experience for me at a young age. It opened my eyes up to become what I am today, why I act the way I am today."

He spent weekdays with the Walkers, weekends with his mother, and in LeBron's fifth-grade year at Portage Path Elementary, he had perfect attendance and excellent grades, and began playing basketball at Summit Lake Community Center.

"LeBron has the knack of fitting in anywhere," said Frank Walker. "He liked the routine of our house. He learns things quick."

Pam Walker said LeBron wasn't the one who needed to be pushed to study. "That was our son, Frankie. We talked to LeBron and all our kids about school, and LeBron liked school."

After his fifth-grade year with the Walkers, LeBron became a solid student, averaging at least a "B" all the way through high school.

Psychologists say that people tend to react to chaos in one of two ways:

1. They treat chaos as normal. In fact, when life is calm it feels strange and so they often create situations involving conflict or extreme change.

2. They seek order. Because so little in their lives

**THE LEBRON FILE**
In 2004, LeBron got the idea for his annual bikeathon for kids after he spent the summer riding his bike with friends to stay in shape in the off-season.

**They moved often and didn't always live together, but there was never anyone closer to LeBron than his mother, Gloria.**

is under control, they try to control whatever they can. They keep their rooms neat. They dress neatly. They grab on to any sort of schedule just so they can have a sense of what is coming next.

"LeBron will do what is necessary to adapt to his circumstances," said Pam Walker. "He wants to be liked. For example, he ate about anything I'd give him. There was once an article about how he loved my German chocolate cake. He did. But he loved pies and other cakes that I made. He even liked to eat broccoli!"

The Walkers say LeBron enjoyed getting his hair cut by Frank Walker in the bathroom. He enjoyed going out to eat about anywhere they chose. He often spent the weekends with his mother, "and there was really no strain" in terms of managing the schedule, Pam Walker said. By Sunday night, LeBron was ready to be back with the Walkers and to go to school.

Gloria James said she "never had to spank LeBron." Those who knew LeBron when he was younger are not surprised by that. He was not perfect, but some children are "strong willed," and others willingly listen to adults who seem to have their best interest at heart.

When LeBron was about to start the sixth grade, Gloria James found an apartment, and he moved back in with her.

Pam Walker said that when LeBron was in the sixth grade, he stayed with his mother during the week, but was often at the Walker home on weekends. That pattern continued for years. The Walkers really were a family to him. So were many of his high school teammates, along with Coach Dru Joyce II and his son, Dru Joyce III.

It's not uncommon for children from single-parent homes to gravitate to larger families, especially if they are made to feel accepted. LeBron did; it was natural for him to blend in. You can see it in his professional life as he works to make new Cleveland Cavaliers teammates feel comfortable — and enjoys mentoring rookies. He seems to remember what it was like to feel like an outsider and to need support from others.

These days, the Walkers go to nearly every Cavaliers game.

"I remind my wife that we were in the gym watching LeBron when no one else was around," said Frank Walker. "Now, we still watch him — only everyone else is watching him, too."

## MVP SEASON MOMENTS

The Cavs went 39-2 at home in 2008-09, and the fans fully embraced the team and its superstar.

## Chapter 3. "All Four of Us"

Dru Joyce III was only 13 years old when he made a decision that would change the lives of so many people. "Little Dru" was perhaps 5-foot-2 when standing on his toes, and maybe 110 pounds if he had five pounds worth of change in his pockets.

He didn't know that within a few years, his father, Dru Joyce II, would become the head basketball coach at Akron's St. Vincent-St. Mary High School, something too much for even his father to dream of.

He didn't know that Keith Dambrot, a part-time basketball clinic coach, would become the head coach at the University of Akron, which seemed utterly impossible.

He didn't know that his friend LeBron James would become the top pick in the 2003 NBA draft, and the most valuable player in the NBA by the age of 24.

He didn't know that he himself would become the starting point guard on nation's top-ranked high school basketball team for the 2002–03 season, or that he'd play four years at the University of Akron for Dambrot, breaking the school's all-time assist record.

All Dru Joyce III knew was that he wanted a coach who wouldn't look down on his talent and his desire, even if the man had to bend down to look Little Dru in the eye.

This story begins on Sunday nights in the late 1990s at Akron's Jewish Community Center, where a former Division I coach named Keith Dambrot was running clinics for just about anyone who wanted to play some hoops. Dambrot was in his fifth year of exile, fired by Central Michigan University after

**LeBron rose to incredible heights at St. V., but he never would have gone to school there had it not been for his undersized best friend.**

using a racial slur in a team meeting. Dambrot had explained that the word was used in a special context and the players were not offended. And nearly all of the players appealed to the university to keep Dambrot. Still, Dambrot was fired. Worse than that, he was labeled a racist by some who didn't bother to check into the story. Now the man who had been a successful head coach at Ashland University and at Tiffin University, an assistant coach at Eastern Michigan University and then head coach at Central Michigan — all before the age of 35 — could not find a coaching job anywhere. He came home to Akron, and worked during the day selling stocks and bonds, and handling investments for Smith Barney in Akron. He applied for coaching positions at some of the worst basketball programs in Northeast Ohio, hoping someone would give him a chance. For five years, no one did. The Jewish Community Center did allow Dambrot to coach kids on Sunday nights. That was his only outlet.

PLAIN DEALER PHOTOGRAPH | JOHN KUNTZ

Dru Joyce II, a sales representative for a food company, had been coaching a summer basketball team called the Shooting Stars for several years, along with Lee Cotton, a truck driver for Federal Express. They were two guys with full-time jobs who were coaching for good reasons — to help kids and to be around their sons. Cotton's son Sian was a wide-bodied center on the team whose best sport was football. Joyce loved basketball and wanted to one day be a head coach on the high school level. For now, he was coaching his son, Dru Joyce III — Little Dru — on the Shooting Stars and also helping out as an assistant coach at Buchtel High in the Akron public school system.

Two other kids on the Shooting Stars were like brothers to Sian Cotton and Little Dru. Their names were Willie McGee and LeBron James. They all came together in the fifth grade. LeBron's and McGee's biological fathers were not living with them. LeBron was living much of the time with the Walker family, and most weekends with his mother, Gloria. McGee was living with his brother and sister in-law after moving to Akron from Chicago, where his mother was having some personal struggles. Both boys longed for a stable family, for a strong male presence. Cotton and Joyce II supplied it.

The Joyce family could not get enough of basketball. They had heard about Dambrot's clinics at the Jewish Community Center, and one Sunday night when Little Dru was in the seventh grade, he showed up with his father to see what the former college coach was teaching.

"The first time I saw Little Dru, I loved the kid," said Dambrot. "You could see his passion for the game. He also was a very sound fundamental player."

A few weeks later, another player came with the Joyce family. He was a slim seventh-grader, about 6-foot with large hands and a graceful way of walking across the floor. Looking at this junior high school kid, you had a feeling that unlike nearly everyone else in junior high, he never had an uncoordinated moment in his life. He didn't move; he *flowed*.

He was LeBron James.

"I remember LeBron at 13 being about 6-foot-1, a spongy guy who wanted to be accepted. He wanted to learn and was willing to listen," said Dambrot. "But at that age, no one knew he'd become a great pro player."

Soon Sian and Lee Cotton were coming to the Sunday night clinics, too. So was Willie McGee. Dambrot knew McGee's older brother, Illya, who had played basketball at the University of Akron; Dambrot's mother had been a professor at the school, and had tutored Illya McGee.

LeBron was the most gifted athlete, but Dambrot's favorite was Little Dru. When he wanted a player to demonstrate a certain technique or drill, he usually selected Dru.

"When I first had Little Dru, I remember him working so hard; he was almost stoic," said Dambrot. "He did every drill. You could see the great training that his mom and dad gave him."

Having coached at the Division I college level, Dambrot valued court savvy as much as pure athleticism. The great ones had both. Some good ones had only average talent, but exceptional basketball intelligence. That was Little Dru. Something else was happening here: Dambrot knew how Dru felt. Like Dru, the 5-foot-8 Dambrot usually was the smallest kid on any team, and was often overlooked and underrated by his coaches.

During the first year that the four friends from the Shooting Stars went to those Sunday workouts, Dambrot was still looking for a coaching job. Then, as they entered the eighth grade, Dambrot

**THE LEBRON FILE**
LeBron was the first person selected three times as Ohio's "Mr. Basketball" (the best player in the state, selected by the Ohio High School Basketball Coaches Association)— in 2001, 2002 and 2003. In his freshman season he was named MVP of the state tournament, an honor he won again in 2002 and 2003.

Romeo Travis    Willie McGee    LeBron James    Sian Cotton    Dru Joyce III

They called themselves the Fab 5. They bonded on the football field, the basketball court and the classroom during their emotional and successful high school years.

TOP: PLAIN DEALER PHOTOGRAPH | ROADELL HICKMAN; BOTTOM: PATTY BURDON, ST. VINCENT–ST. MARY HIGH SCHOOL

was hired as the head coach at an Akron private school, St. Vincent-St. Mary. Some of the school's board members knew Dambrot and his family. They knew he was a good man who'd made a mistake. They knew he had been coaching kids for free for years. And they decided that he deserved a second chance. Besides, his salary would be only $3,000. (He was not going to teach there; his living would still come from the investment business.) If it didn't work out, they could fire him and all it would cost would be $3,000. It was a good opportunity for them, too. They knew they could put a major college coach on their bench for $3,000, and stabilize a basketball program that had been through some recent highs and lows.

The new job started out well. In his first season, Dambrot coached the St. Vincent-St. Mary Irish to the regionals of the state tournament, a real boost for the school. It would

**LeBron as a freshman.**

soon get even better — far better than he could imagine.

"I really thought Little Dru and the rest of them were going to Buchtel [High]," said Dambrot. "Big Dru [Joyce II] was an assistant coach at Buchtel. They lived close to the school. It seemed like a natural."

Buchtel, a predominantly black public high school on Akron's west side, had the strongest athletic program of any of the city's eight public high schools. The school routinely sent football and basketball players to Division I college programs.

Still, Dambrot tried to sell the Joyce family on the merits of St. Vincent-St. Mary. The school was well-known for its academics, and several Akron area civic business leaders were among its alumni. And although its enrollment was 90 percent white, the parochial school had been recruiting minorities. It was also located near downtown Akron.

"The four of us made a promise that we'd all go to the same high school together, and we'd all stick

it out," said LeBron. "We were not going to let girls, school, sports, anything get between us."

But which high school would it be?

Buchtel was pushing hard for all four of them, but Little Dru sensed their real target was LeBron.

"I thought Buchtel would write me off because of my size," said Dru. "All four of us liked St. V. with Coach Dambrot being there, but none of us said anything."

The Joyce family had a meeting. Little Dru explained that while he understood why his dad, being an assistant coach at Buchtel, would want him to go there, he had a bad feeling about his chances to play there. He believed Dambrot liked him and "would give me a fair shot. That's all I want."

"Little Dru thought he'd get lost in the shuffle at Buchtel," said Dambrot. "He knew I was a coach who'd really work with him. Then it became interesting because they [the Buchtel coaches] were working on Gloria James, trying to convince her [to send LeBron to Buchtel]. But she stayed firm in the whole thing ... I think she has a tremendous commitment to her son, and really did want what was best for him."

Buchtel was an inner-city public school with a solid record of sending players to college, especially in football. Furthermore, its mostly black community was very proud of its athletic tradition, and there was real pressure on Dru Joyce II and Lee Cotton to send their sons to Buchtel — with the assumption being that LeBron would follow.

Going to St. Vincent-St. Mary was perceived by some local residents as a betrayal of Akron's inner city. That didn't discourage Little Dru.

"I said that I was going to St. V.," he said. "The other guys followed."

Dru had been the point guard on their summer teams. He was a natural leader. He had tremen-

**LeBron started dunking in seventh grade. By high school, all the hype had him posing.**

PLAIN DEALER PHOTOGRAPH | MARVIN FONG

dous respect for his father, but he also had the guts to explain his reasons for not wanting to attend Buchtel.

"When Little Dru said he was coming to St. V., it took some of the pressure off LeBron," said Dambrot. "Everyone knew that he'd follow the other guys. All he had to do was say, 'I'm going with my friends.' And Gloria also thought it was a good idea."

St. Vincent-St. Mary, a Catholic school, probably would not have been LeBron's first choice. His good friend Frankie Walker (son of Pam and Frank Walker) had chosen to attend Buchtel. But his three closest friends — Dru Joyce III, Willie McGee and Sian Cotton — had even a stronger pull on his heart. Ten years later when receiving his MVP award, LeBron looked into the audience, saw Dru Joyce II and said, "I had no biological father around to teach me to tie my shoes, fold my clothes ... that man helped me with a lot of things that a father would."

Think of how LeBron moved from place to place to place when he was younger. Think of how he lived with the Walker family for nearly two years, and how he worked so hard to fit in. Think of how he enjoyed just having people around him whom he could trust, people who had not only said the right things, but had lived the right way. Think of a kid who wanted peace and structure, and how he found it with this group. It was Little Dru who had to make a tough decision. For LeBron and McGee — another kid longing for that male influence — it was easy to follow their point guard.

# Chapter 4. St. V.

In the moments before LeBron James' first high school game on December 3, 1999, head coach Keith Dambrot was pacing back and forth. His mouth was dry, his throat a bit tight. His Akron St. Vincent-St. Mary High School team was playing in a half-filled gym in Cuyahoga Falls. One college coach in particular was in the stands — Bob Huggins, of the University of Cincinnati. Huggins had coached at the University of Akron and had already heard about LeBron; he wanted an early edge in recruiting. LeBron, who was about 6-foot-1 when Dambrot first saw him as a seventh grader was now 6-foot-4, 170 pounds. He already had a Division I basketball build at the age of 14.

"I never felt more pressure in my life than coaching LeBron," said Dambrot. "Even as a freshman, I knew that it wouldn't be long before he'd never have to worry where his next meal would be coming from. He was going to be a pro, make a lot of money. It was just a matter of if he had to go to college first. I felt pressure to make sure he did the right things, on and off the court. I also had to push him to a level where he could achieve quickly."

Dambrot had a 16-9 record in his first season at the school. His approach, he said, was to "coach the kids as if it were a college team." The practices would be intense and disciplined. St. Vincent-St. Mary stressed academics in the classroom, and Dambrot planned to do the same in the gym and the locker room. The kids would do more than just play the game; they'd *think* the game. They'd be prepared for college basketball the same way an honor student in math takes a few college level courses while still in high school to get a taste of

**Coach Keith Dambrot knew LeBron could be a superstar — he just didn't want to mess it up.**

what life will be like at the university level.

LeBron has said he was shocked by the Dambrot who coached him and the rest of the Shooting Stars that first season. The patient teacher he knew from the Jewish Community Center was now coaching at the top of his lungs, jumping on every mistake. He had never been coached like this before.

Dambrot admitted, "I was probably harder on LeBron than anyone else in the program. The reason was I thought he was the best player ... and he had the most to lose if I didn't coach him right. I set the ground rules early."

Dambrot had a meeting with LeBron early in their first season together.

"LeBron, I'll coach you any way you want," Dambrot said. "Do you want me to sugar-coat it, or do you want me to tell the truth?"

LeBron said, "I want the truth."

So then it was up to LeBron to handle the truth.

"Whenever I said something to LeBron that he didn't like, I'd remind him, 'You told me that you wanted the truth,'" said Dambrot.

Dambrot had four freshmen in Dru Joyce III,

**LeBron and the Irish played several national powers, including Oak Hill Academy three times.**

PLAIN DEALER PHOTOGRAPH | ROADELL HICKMAN

Sian Cotton, Willie McGee and LeBron, all of whom had been the stars not only of local youth leagues, but had been a powerhouse in regional summer AAU tournaments played in different parts of the country. It had come pretty easy for them. They had solid coaching — especially for grade school kids — from Dru Joyce II and Lee Cotton, who both knew the game and also supplied a father's steady hand to all the players. In the case of LeBron, he was physically superior to almost any kid he faced, anywhere, anytime.

Dambrot also had seniors on his team such as Maverick Carter and John Taylor, good players who he knew should be in the spotlight in their final seasons. Yet the talk was about the four freshmen, especially LeBron. Dambrot continually told the freshmen, "You're not as good as you think you are ... you really haven't done anything yet ... you have a lot to learn."

On and on it went, day after day.

He seemed to be nitpicking them to distraction, but Dambrot knew that the little things could make a big difference for any player who had huge hoop dreams. Not only did Dambrot see his mission as preparing LeBron for an eventual pro career, but he desperately wanted Dru Joyce III to reach his goal of being a Division I college point guard. At this time, Joyce III was a 5-foot-2 freshman who looked like he'd never be taller than 5-foot-6. If he did become a part of a major college program, it would be to hand the towels to the real players and wash the uniforms after games.

It was only later the four freshmen realized that they were blessed to have had Dambrot as a coach. How many high school kids are coached by someone who had been at the Division I university level? This is not a knock at Buchtel or any other school that LeBron could have attended, but where else would he have been in practice each day with a coach who knew exactly what it took to play major college basketball? Most high school coaches spent their careers in high school coaching, or perhaps some time at a small college. Very, very few were head coaches at the top collegiate level.

Furthermore, LeBron was coached by someone who was not intimidated by his talent, someone who didn't fear that LeBron would become upset about something at practice, storm out of the gym and transfer to another school. Then there were Lee Cotton and Dru Joyce II at every practice, two men who LeBron knew loved and cared about him. If they went along with Dambrot's approach, LeBron had to take it seriously. A lot of coaches are afraid to criticize a great player, be it in high school or college. They fear the player will quit and find another coach who won't be as demanding. Then the coach would look bad to his school and its supporters because he could not keep the great player happy. When the great player leaves, the school does not win as much. And that makes life even worse for the coach, who could lose his job. It's easier to just sweetly support the star. But Dambrot refused to do that. Just as important, Lee Cotton and Dru Joyce II stood firmly with their head coach — when it would have been a temptation for other fathers/assistants to undercut his authority.

"That was key," said Dambrot. "They gave me tremendous support. Something else most people don't know is LeBron also lived with the Joyce family for a while. What they thought was important to LeBron."

If you focus solely on one of Dambrot's outbursts in practice or a tirade during a timeout during a game, it's likely you'll miss the big picture. Dambrot is often both the good and bad cop, sometimes within 15 minutes of each other. He'll yell at a player at the start of practice, then put his arm around the same player and speak quietly to him after practice is over. Dru Joyce III understood exactly what Dambrot was doing. The little point guard knew the coach had a huge heart that pounded with a burning desire to win big and make all the players better. Some of the Irish players resented the fact that Dambrot didn't yell as much at Joyce III as the others, but as LeBron realized, that was because Dru did things correctly the first time. Because he was small, Dru could not rely on his natu-

**THE LEBRON FILE**
LeBron scored 40 points or more in a high school game six times — five times in his senior season.

**Dru Joyce III and LeBron had a natural friendship that carried over to the court.**

ral ability to prevail. He had to pay more attention than most players, as LeBron did when he followed Little Dru to St. Vincent-St. Mary, and began to follow the point guard's example on the court.

"LeBron helped me be a better player, but I also helped him be a better player," said Dru.

Dambrot agreed, adding, "Little Dru believed that, in his own way, he was as good as LeBron. He never gave LeBron an inch."

While LeBron and some of the other players from that 1999–2000 season seemed to loathe playing for Dambrot, by the end of the year they were 27–0 and had won a state title. They were not only physically stronger than their opponents, they were mentally tougher. They made adjustments on offense and defense quickly. They didn't wilt under pressure. They truly played as a team.

"When LeBron was a freshman, he had only a 24-inch vertical leap," said Dambrot. "That was not anything close to what he has now. I knew that in the next few years, he was going to be jumping even

higher. His skill level was phenomenal. His mental ability was phenomenal. I think he would have been a pro if he stayed at 6-foot-4, 170 pounds. Not dominating like today, but still a good pro."

Before LeBron's sophomore season, he attended the Five-Star Camp, a legendary talent showcase for high school players founded and run by Howard Garfinkel. In 2000, Garfinkel talked about all the great players who attended his camp over the years — Stephon Marbury, Grant Hill, Rasheed Wallace, Elton Brand and others.

"LeBron played as well or better than any of them when they were sophomores at my camp," Garfinkel said. "It was ridiculous; he totally dominated. I've never seen anything quite like it. He can shoot it. He can pass it. He knows the game."

LeBron was on the summer all-star circuit, playing in tournaments in Utah, Las Vegas, Memphis, Orlando and the Five-Star camp in Pittsburgh. All of this at the age of 15.

Dru Joyce II remembers how LeBron cried the

first time when he was on an airplane. That was when he was 11, and the Shooting Stars were playing in an AAU tournament in Salt Lake City, Utah. On the first leg of the trip from Cleveland to Houston, LeBron was terrified, tears pouring down his face. He settled down on the second part, after they switched planes in Houston. By the time he was 16, LeBron had already logged more miles than some traveling salesmen who were gold card members of their frequent flier clubs.

Already, more than 100 colleges had written him — every major program in the country.

Little Dru remembered LeBron as a "child prodigy. LeBron was always bigger and better than anyone else. He never went through a stage where he was clumsy."

As a sophomore, LeBron was listing himself at 6-foot-6 ½, the same size as Michael Jordan. That probably was accurate. His arms seemed long enough to touch the clouds. His hands were big, but nimble with long, strong fingers that made it so easy for him to catch and throw passes. Small hands can be a real negative when playing a game with a big ball. Heading into his sophomore year, he had a 2.8 grade point average and no real discipline problems. His grades were the best of the four Shooting Stars. In that sophomore season, the Irish were 27-1 and won another state title.

That year, Steve Culp joined the coaching staff, bringing even more college credentials. He had been an assistant at Cleveland State University and the University of Akron for a total of four years. His last job before joining Dambrot was as the head coach at Akron Firestone High. It was as if LeBron and the rest of the players were getting a graduate degree in basketball while still in high school.

"Early in his freshman year, I knew LeBron was going to a major college and then to the NBA," said Dambrot. "Three games into his sophomore year, I knew he'd never see college. He was headed right to the NBA."

Former Cleveland Cavaliers General Manager Jim Paxson first saw LeBron as a sophomore, and he later agreed with Dambrot: "The first thing that struck me was his passing ability. He had great vi-

sion. He made a length-of-the-court bounce pass — foul line to foul line [about 70 feet] — and hit a player right in stride. Good NBA players can't make that pass, and he was doing it as a sophomore in high school ... You could see how he was figuring it out from night to night, what he needed to do to win — score, pass, rebound."

This was the ideal spot for LeBron to be nurtured and bloom. Nowhere else would all these elements of great coaching, familiar father figures, friends on the team, solid teachers who expected proper behavior and academic competence come together for a fatherless young man who has always longed for stability and family. He responded well to structure, and there was plenty of that at his high school.

"I can't take credit for something that was very important to LeBron's success," said Dambrot. "He was *always* a good teammate. He knew he was better than everyone else, but he never acted like it. He got his teammates involved, he didn't care what he scored if we won big. He was happy to pass off and let the other guys score. [Former Cavalier] Dajuan Wagner was scoring 100 points [in a blowout for Camden (N.J.) High School], and LeBron was scoring 12 against Crestview High when he could have coasted to 50. He was like Magic Johnson in that respect. The maturity level was unbelievable. It showed he really did care about his teammates — he didn't just talk about it like some guys."

That draws back upon LeBron's desire to fit in, be it with the Walkers, with the Joyce and Cotton families or with the Shooting Stars. Being a good friend and having respect for adults came naturally to him. The same was true of his unselfish approach to basketball.

"When LeBron was 11, he really liked to shoot the ball — a lot," said Dru Joyce II, adding that LeBron's dribbling skills were raw. He was taller than most kids, but had to turn his back to them and kind of muscle his way to the rim to score. He didn't look to pass to his teammates, and they stood around and watched.

"It was not how I taught them to play," said Joyce. "One day, we were driving down East Avenue [in Akron], and I started telling LeBron about passing the ball — and how great players made their teammates better. I talked to him about getting his shots in the flow of a game."

Joyce doubted that an 11-year-old LeBron would understand. He assumed this would be the first of many discussions on the same topic.

"That was the last time that I ever had to talk to LeBron about shooting too much," he said. "He just got it. He started passing the ball."

Lee Cotton remembered that time, adding, "LeBron quickly came to know that he needed a group of core guys to help him. We stressed he couldn't do everything. He needed Little Dru to hit that outside shot. He needed big Sian [Cotton] to clear the lane, get some rebounds. LeBron liked that idea, liked being a part of the team."

Former Irish assistant coach Steve Culp said, "Know what our biggest problem with LeBron was? Sometimes, we had to get him to shoot more in some games. He liked to pass off and let the other kids score. He never cared that some people were telling him that he should score more points. He was confident enough in his own game to ignore that."

Joyce II added, "That's true. We had to get him to take more shots in some games. LeBron was dedicated to team basketball."

LeBron averaged 18 points per game as a freshman, 25 as a sophomore, 29 as a junior, and 31 as a senior.

"He averaged 20 as a rookie in the NBA," said Culp. "That tells you he could have averaged 50 or more if he wanted to in high school."

During LeBron's freshman year, Joyce II explained, "I had pretty much taught LeBron all that I could. Getting Keith Dambrot was important because he had been a head coach in college and helped LeBron grow to a new level."

But that also was true of Joyce II, who spent two years learning from a college coach, being at Dam-

**THE LEBRON FILE**
The fewest points LeBron scored in a game in high school was 11, in his third game as a freshman, against Akron Garfield High School.

The most points LeBron scored in a high school game was 52, in his senior season against Westchester High School from Los Angeles.

brot's side in every practice, every game, every half-time and pregame talk, every planning session. Joyce II often paid his way into coaching clinics to grow as a coach. Now, he was learning every day — and being prepared to take over as head coach.

The Irish had become one of the elite high school teams in the country. They had a shoe contract from adidas. The company supplied uniforms, warm-ups, gym bags, sweatsuits and gym bags — thousands of dollars' worth of goods for free. Gloria James often wore adidas shoes and sweatsuits.

"Some people said we got that because I was a college coach," said Dambrot. "When I was at Central Michigan, I struggled to get a shoe contract."

In this case, adidas came to him.

"One reason — LeBron," said Dambrot.

At the age of 15, shoe companies were already recruiting a player whom they hoped would be the next Michael Jordan. It also became a tremendous drawing card for local athletes who not only wanted to play with LeBron, but also get that equipment. In 2000, St. Vincent-St. Mary was the only Akron area high school with a shoe contract. It also was the only one ready to embark on a national schedule against some of the best teams in the country. The Irish with LeBron were just too good to stay home, Dambrot believed.

After LeBron's sophomore season, Dambrot was hired as an assistant coach at the University of Akron. Dru Joyce II took over as head coach of the Irish, with Lee Cotton and Steve Culp remaining as assistants. While some of the players — including LeBron — were upset that Dambrot left, the parts for success for LeBron were in place. Practice habits were ingrained, expectations had been set. Joyce II was now ready to be a high school head coach, although it would have been hard for any coach to get everything right in the next two years as the hype about LeBron bubbled over. As a junior, LeBron and the Irish were upset in the finals of the state playoffs. The following season, they came back to not only win the state title — the third in four years for LeBron — but they also were the No. 1 ranked team in the country by USA Today. They appeared on national television. In the middle of LeBron's junior season, he was being projected as a lottery pick, probably in the top five of the 2003 draft. By the start of his senior season, he was the consensus No. 1 projected pick for the 2003 NBA draft.

Not everything went smoothly. There were well-documented controversies. One was when Gloria James secured a loan to buy her son an expensive Hummer H2 sport utility vehicle — while still living in publicly subsidized housing. The loan was against LeBron's future earnings (all any auto dealer had to do was pick up a sports page and know that within six months, LeBron would be worth millions). Then, LeBron was suspended for two games for accepting two jerseys from a sporting goods store in exchange for signing some photographs for them to put on the wall. LeBron also went through a period when he seemed disgruntled over the fact that the school was taking advantage of his fame, receiving thousands of dollars in guarantees to play in different tournaments around the country because promoters knew LeBron would be a huge gate attraction. That was especially true after he appeared on the cover of Sports Illustrated as a junior. The magazine dubbed him "The Chosen One," suggesting LeBron was on the way to being the next Michael Jordan. At first, LeBron gladly signed every cover for adults or children. Then he discovered some of those autographed magazine covers were showing up on eBay and being sold for hundreds of dollars. After that, he signed only for kids.

Now, looking in the rearview mirror, those episodes seem like fairly minor indiscretions, especially compared to the enormous legal problems and other personal issues that often afflict other young star athletes — most of whom don't face anywhere near the national scrutiny LeBron James did even as a teenager.

"Think of all the guys who had special talents and flushed them down the toilet," said Dambrot. "It's a fine line, and once you make a wrong turn, it's over.

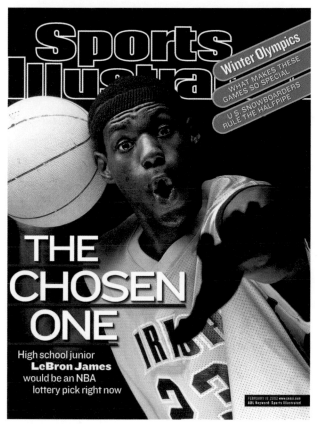

LeBron has been on the cover of more than a dozen different national magazines including Sports Illustrated, ESPN The Magazine, Vogue, GQ, Forbes, Men's Fitness, Men's Health, Black Enterprise, Parade, The Sporting News and SLAM.

I made a mistake [at Central Michigan] and it really cost me. I remember having talks with LeBron about girls, about drugs, about working hard. I felt pressure to get him to do the right things."

So did Dru Joyce II, Lee Cotton and Steve Culp. The coaching staff knew they had a once-in-a-generation athlete, and they remain proud of LeBron to this day because he didn't waste his talent or his opportunities. Culp, and especially Cotton, have never received the full credit they deserve for LeBron's success. Cotton was always supportive of the head coach — Joyce II or Dambrot. He drove vans taking players to games. He washed uniforms. As Dambrot said, "Lee was always there for whatever you needed. He's a great guy." Culp has an excellent grasp of the game because

## MVP SEASON MOMENTS

In leading the Cavs to a team record 66 wins, LeBron brought the crowd to its feet to "witness" his play.

PLAIN DEALER PHOTOGRAPH | JOHN KUNTZ

of his four years as a Division I college assistant.

"You are always asking yourself if you were doing the right thing for all the kids, not just LeBron," said Joyce II. "There was tremendous pressure to win. And when we won, it was because of the kids. If we lost, it was because Keith was no longer the coach. I understood that."

More important, Joyce II overcame the stigma of being "LeBron's coach." He won a state title with LeBron, another title in 2009 for the Irish.

"Being around LeBron has made a lot of people better," said Dambrot. "If I had good teams but no LeBron, I'd probably still be the coach at St. V. Or maybe an assistant somewhere. But I doubt I'd be a head coach at the Division I level."

Dambrot was hired as an assistant in 2001 at the University of Akron, promoted to head coach in 2004. He was the only Division I coach to offer Dru Joyce III a scholarship, and the point guard not only started for the Zips, but set the school's all-time assist record.

"Suppose Little Dru had decided to go to Buchtel, and the other players followed," said Dambrot. "LeBron still would have gone into the NBA. But Buchtel could not have played such a national schedule because they were in a league. LeBron and the others would not have faced such strong competition. That really created LeBron James, in terms of all the national marketing."

Dambrot's point is that a Most Valuable Player really does make others around him better.

"Because Little Dru went to St. V., Big Dru ends up coaching at that school," said Dambrot. "That's the only way it happens. Because I coached LeBron and won a lot of games, Akron decided to give me another chance at college coaching. Because if you coached LeBron and your program has a shoe deal with LeBron's company and about every kid wants to be like LeBron — that helps you attract players as a coach. I am able to take Little Dru with me, and he becomes a terrific college player. Even on the NBA level, Mike Brown [Cleveland Cavaliers' Head Coach] got a chance to coach LeBron and be the NBA's [2009] Coach of the Year. LeBron has changed a lot of lives for the better."

# Chapter 5. **Football**

"I'm telling you, LeBron just loves football," said Jay Brophy, who coached him in that sport at St. Vincent-St. Mary.

That's right: LeBron played football at St. Vincent-St. Mary. *Three years* of football. He played enough football to be an all-state receiver by his junior season. He played enough football that he could have been "picked the best football player in Ohio if he had played as a senior."

Those words came from Mark Murphy — a 12-year NFL pro who later served as LeBron's assistant football coach with the Irish.

LeBron played enough football that Brophy — a four-year NFL pro — is convinced he could have been a Division I college quarterback, even though he never played that position in a high school game.

"He could throw a football at least 60 yards," said Brophy.

"I saw him throw it 70 yards," said Murphy. "In practice, we sometimes used him as our scout-team quarterback to get our defense ready for games. He was quick, had a really strong arm and he was tall enough to see over the linemen."

But there is another reason Brophy and Murphy are convinced LeBron could have been a Big Ten quarterback.

"His *mind*," said Murphy. "You'd tell him something once, and he'd remember it. He knew offensive formations. He knew defensive formations. He knew the patterns he was supposed to run, and the patterns other receivers would run. He knew how the defense would react."

Remember, this is a former NFL defensive back talking, not some starstruck young high school

**LeBron's first love was football. Some say he was a good enough wide receiver to play in the NFL.**

coach who had never been around elite athletic talent before. There were two reasons LeBron didn't play quarterback. The first was he was an elite basketball talent, and there is more risk of injury for a long-legged quarterback being blinded-sided on a tackle than at receiver. Another was that Willie McGee — a member of the Shooting Stars — was also the quarterback, and a good one.

"But no question, LeBron could play the position," said Murphy.

By the middle of LeBron's sophomore year, Brophy said, he had received letters and calls "from every major college in the country" about LeBron. They wanted to recruit him as a receiver. Brophy said virtually all the top-ranked teams were intrigued by a 6-foot-6 wide receiver who could outjump any defensive back and caught nearly everything he touched, as if he had suction cups for fingers.

"They'd put two or three guys on him, and LeBron would still make big catches," said Brophy. "I saw him becoming something like Harold Carmichael and Randy Moss [both NFL receivers]. I heard some people say he'd make a good tight end. But I wanted him at receiver — who can defend him on a lob into the end zone?"

PLAIN DEALER PHOTOGRAPH | PHIL LONG

LeBron's first love was football. It was on a football field for the South Side Rangers as a fourth grader that Frank Walker first spotted him. It was on those same youth football fields that Romeo Travis — later a high school teammate of LeBron and a star at the University of Akron — first met.

"I first played against him when we were about eight," said Travis. "He was a running back, and he was huge — the biggest kid on the field. When they gave him the ball, it seemed like he scored about every time. It was ridiculous."

In his early years of elementary school, LeBron played more football than basketball. He was on a flag football team in grade school, but mostly it was pickup games with his friends. He enjoyed watching football on television, which was not always the case with basketball. By the time he was in high school, he had become a fan of Florida State and the Dallas Cowboys. The reason was simple: They were generally the best teams in the early-to-mid 1990s. Many of their games were on national television. With the Cleveland Browns inactive from 1996–99, the prime years of LeBron's pre-high school youth, he watched what was on nationally each week. Some people would later criticize him for rooting for the Cowboys and not the home-team Browns. But he grew up watching the Cowboys. And when LeBron dreamed of playing college football as a kid, he wanted to play for Florida State.

In fact, when he tried out for high school football as a freshman, LeBron wasn't sure what was his best sport — football or basketball. St. Vincent-St. Mary basketball coach Keith Dambrot thought hoops would be his future, but Dambrot had not seen LeBron in football. That first high school football season, Jim Meyer was the varsity coach. LeBron made the freshman team, then was promoted to the junior varsity. By the end of the season, he was with the varsity and caught eight passes in the final game of the season.

"You could see the talent right away," said Meyer.

**THE LEBRON FILE**
LeBron was the first basketball player to be named Gatorade Player of the Year twice and the first to be named to the USA Today All-American team for three straight years.

"I'd like to say that our coaching helped him progress that fast as a receiver, but he did things you can't coach. He'd go down the field, and if you got the ball near him, he caught it."

As a sophomore, he was back on the football field, an immediate varsity starter at wide receiver. LeBron had 42 receptions for 820 yards and seven touchdowns. It was after that season that LeBron started to get all the attention for football. Some recruiting publications listed him as the No. 1 wide receiver prospect in Ohio at the age of 16.

"I give LeBron a ton of credit for playing football," said Meyer, who was LeBron's head coach for his first two football seasons. "There is so much pressure on high school kids to concentrate on one sport, to specialize. Only one out of 100 high school athletes will receive any type of athletic scholarship. It really should be part of the high school experience, being on different teams with your friends. That was part of the reason he played."

Indeed it was, as Willie McGee and Sian Cotton also were on the football team. The only member of the core group of the Shooting Stars who didn't play football was Dru Joyce III. The point guard was 5-foot-2 and less than 100 pounds as a freshman. Football didn't make sense to him. When Romeo Travis transferred to St. Vincent-St. Mary for his sophomore season, he not only joined LeBron on the court, but also went out for football.

"Keith Dambrot liked his kids to play football," said Meyer. "You have to be tough to play basketball, but it's a different type of mentality for football. You play outside. You get dirty and cold and wet. You have coaches yelling at you. There are people hitting you. You learn about sacrifice and fitting in with a team."

LeBron loved the routine of football, according to his coaches. They insist he "was never late." Brophy recalls LeBron coming early to the Saturday morning Masses on game days, despite LeBron not

**By the time he was a sophomore, LeBron was being recruited by college football programs.**

being a Catholic. It's what the coaches asked the players to do, and LeBron did it.

LeBron won the Ohio Mr. Basketball award as a sophomore. He was the MVP of the ABCD Camp at age 16, outplaying various stars from across the country in different summer basketball camps. After that summer, the James family decided he'd skip college and enter the NBA after his senior season. They never announced it, but that was the plan. It was obvious that millions of dollars awaited LeBron as a basketball player.

"There was a lot of pressure on LeBron not to play as a junior," said Brophy. "They didn't want him to get hurt. That was understandable. But he missed his friends. He was hanging around practices, even though he wasn't playing."

LeBron did not dress with the football team for

the opening game of his junior season when the Irish upset Akron's Garfield High School. Wearing his letter jacket, LeBron watched the game from the fence behind the Irish bench, cheering for his friends and teammates. McGee had a great game as the starting quarterback, Sian Cotton excelled as an offensive and defensive lineman and Travis was playing defensive end. Brophy recalls that when the game was over, he climbed over the fence and was on the field, celebrating with the players.

Over that same weekend, the young pop singer Aaliyah died in a plane crash. LeBron was a fan of hers, and the shocking news of her death reminded him that, as he put it, "tomorrow is not guaranteed." (It's something he still often says.) Both the win over Garfield and the singer's sudden death convinced LeBron that he didn't want to miss out

## MVP SEASON MOMENTS

After his alma mater won its fifth state championship, LeBron consoles Thurgood Marshall's Juwan Staten.

on anything important — including football.

"When LeBron told us that he wanted to play, we said that he had missed training camp," said Murphy. "We told him that we had to take it to the seniors and let them vote if he could play."

The seniors all knew and respected LeBron as a talented athlete and good teammate. They quickly voted to bring him back.

"His mom was worried about LeBron playing," said Brophy. "She kept telling me, 'Take care of my baby!' We didn't use LeBron on defense, or run plays for him to catch passes over the middle. We didn't want to get him hurt."

Meyer, Brophy and Murphy all said that football was a place away from all the pressure and notoriety that LeBron had in the basketball arena. He loved going to practice. He took naps on the gym floor before some practices, just like his teammates.

"LeBron was coachable, respectful and he listened," said Murphy. "He just wanted to be one of the guys."

That season, LeBron caught 61 passes for 1,245 yards and 16 touchdowns as a junior in 13 games. The team reached the Division IV state semifinals. He mostly ran fade routes and almost never went over the middle. He also tried to run out of bounds as much as possible. Yes, he was a football player, but he played very carefully. In practice no one was allowed to hit him. All of it was to protect him, of course. The coaches would sometimes take LeBron off the field before a running play. They were afraid that opposing teams might take a cheap shot at him with a low chop block to cut out his legs and possibly injure his knee. Still, he was named first-team All-State in football.

"[Ohio State football coach] Jim Tressel visited our school, not to see LeBron, but to talk about some other players," said Brophy. "LeBron heard that Coach Tressel was there, and he found me and asked me to introduce him to Coach Tressel. I do

think if he had gone to college to play football, it probably would have been at Ohio State."

Tressel did recruit Sian Cotton, who spent two years as a backup lineman with the Ohio State Buckeyes before transferring to another school. Odds are, a football-playing LeBron would have accompanied his buddy to Columbus, had basketball not been such an overpowering lure.

LeBron did break his little finger in football, but that was not why he decided to skip the sport as a senior. Instead, the decision was sealed when he broke his wrist in a spring AAU basketball tournament in Chicago. He was undercut on a dunk attempt and he landed hard on his right wrist. It knocked him out of all-summer basketball. After that sobering injury it was decided for sure that he was not going to play football as a senior.

"LeBron told me that if he hadn't broken the wrist, he was going to play," said Brophy. "I believe him. Being on our team with those guys meant so much to him. I always thought it kind of funny how everyone was so worried about LeBron getting hurt in football, and his only major injury in high school was in basketball. You never really know what will happen."

In case LeBron might change his mind later as a senior, Brophy kept his pads, uniform and even his locker ready. LeBron continued to come to the football field house during the fall to work out because that's where the weights were and because he still wanted to be with his friends. It was also a place to escape some of the pressure from all the agents and shoe companies recruiting him and talking about multimillion-dollar deals.

"I love it when LeBron calls himself a football player while in the NBA," said Brophy. "I do think playing football made him a better basketball player, because he does take a physical beating on the court — and he keeps getting up and playing harder. He can handle all the bumps and bruises better than a lot of guys in that league. Not just because he's big, but it's also because he's tough."

> **THE LEBRON FILE**
> LeBron likes ancient war movies. Among his favorites are "Gladiator," "300," and "Braveheart." He gave his second son, Bryce, the middle name "Maximus" after Russell Crowe's character in "Gladiator."

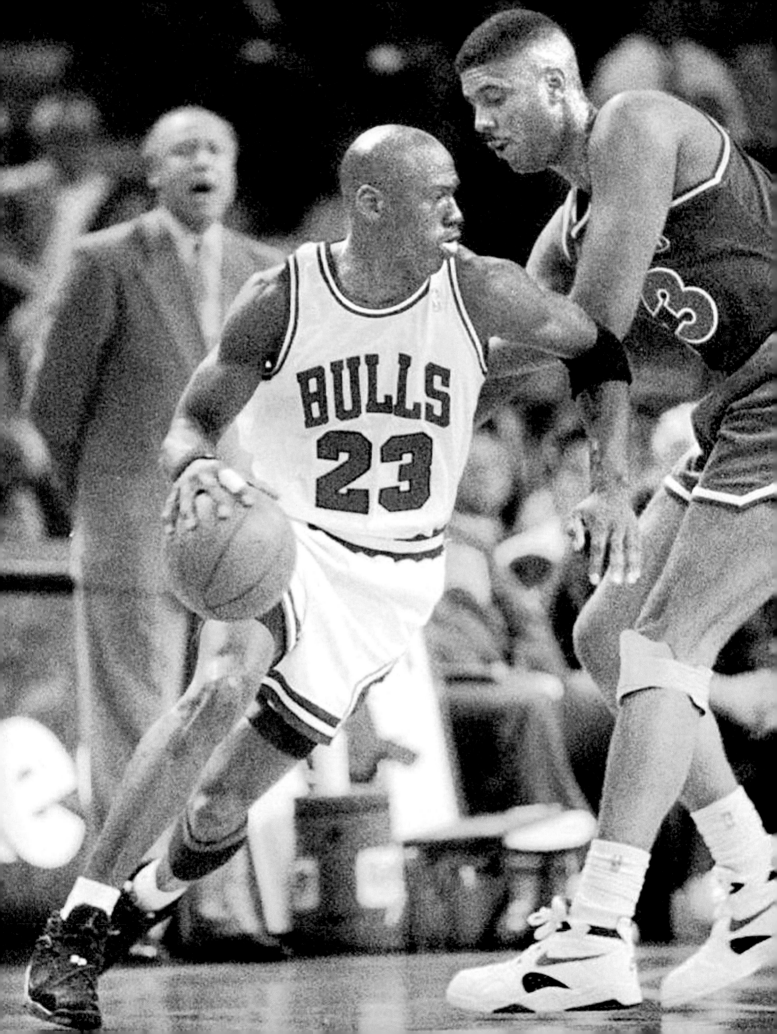

## Chapter 6. The Jordan Influence

LeBron James grew up a Michael Jordan fan, and he has never backed away from comparisons between himself and Jordan, perhaps the great player in NBA history. While he has never said it directly, LeBron, in many ways, clearly wants to be like Mike.

First, a history lesson: LeBron was born on December 30, 1984. It was three months and four days after Jordan played his first regular-season game with the Chicago Bulls (a rather underwhelming 16-point performance in which he had as many turnovers, 5, as field goals). By the time LeBron was 10 years old, Jordan had won three consecutive NBA titles (1991–93) and had three MVP awards next to his name. Larry Bird had retired and Magic Johnson was at the end of his career. There was only one name in the NBA, and it was Jordan. There was only one brand name when it came to shoes — and it was Air Jordan from Nike. There was only one NBA jersey that most kids in the early 1990s wanted to wear — it was Jordan's No. 23.

Some Northeast Ohio fans wonder why LeBron isn't a fan of Cleveland sports teams. They judge LeBron by their own experience. Many have fathers or grandfathers or aunts or mothers who took them to games at the old Cleveland Stadium to watch the Indians and Browns. Some come from families of Cleveland sports fans dating back to when the Indians still played at League Park

**THE LEBRON FILE**
LeBron has made commercials for three different Coca-Cola products: Sprite, Powerade and Vitamin Water.

in the 1930s, or when Cleveland Browns Head Coach Paul Brown making pro football matter right after World War II in the 1940s. Some fans recall when the Cavaliers were born in 1970, and the expansion franchise played at the old Cleveland Arena on Euclid Avenue (where visiting teams were afraid to use the dressing rooms; they would change at a hotel across the street and walk to the arena in their uniforms). Or they had someone in their families to buy tickets to cheer for the Cavaliers at the old Richfield Coliseum. In a number of Cleveland families, names such as Feller, Colavito, Charboneau, McDowell, Rosen and Boudreau are more than men who once played for the Indians. They are like a second set of relatives who are mentioned as part of the family lore. The same with Paul Brown, Jim Brown, Frank Ryan, Gary Collins, Leroy Kelly, Brian Sipe, Bernie Kosar, Reggie Rucker and so many other former Cleveland Browns.

But LeBron had none of that growing up. He had no father to take him to games. Instead, he had a teenaged mother who struggled to keep them in the same apartment for more than a year. He had no one in his home talking about the Cleveland teams, talking about what those games meant to the family. And the state of Cleveland

**As a boy, LeBron's walls were covered with pictures of his idol, Michael Jordan.**

sports in the early 1990s, when LeBron was first paying attention, wasn't impressive. The Indians had been awful for more than three decades. The Browns were coached by a young and inexperienced Bill Belichick, who was hated by most Cleveland fans. Iconic quarterback Bernie Kosar had been cut, and owner Art Modell was plotting to move his losing franchise to Baltimore. If there was no family history with those teams, why would LeBron gravitate in their direction? Only the Cavaliers were winners, but they had a problem. That problem wore No. 23 and played for the Chicago Bulls. Michael Jordan, knocked the Cavs out of the playoffs *four* times — in 1988, '89, '92, and '93. LeBron became a sports fan by watching television, and he adopted the Bulls, the Dallas Cowboys and the Florida State Seminoles football team, and the New York Yankees — the powerhouse teams when he was coming of age as a sports fan.

Like many kids, he wanted Air Jordan shoes. Gloria James could not afford the $100 price tag. But she could buy her son posters and magazines featuring Jordan. LeBron collected anything he could about Jordan, and taped the stuff to his bedroom walls. The Jordan pictures were something that made the various places where he lived feel like home. The walls could change as they kept moving, but he could surround himself with his favorite pictures. After leaving the Walker family in 1995, Pam Walker helped Gloria James find a rent-assisted apartment called Spring Hill in the Akron neighborhood of West Hill. Gloria believed this place would be "home" for a few years, and she was proud that her son would have his own bedroom. LeBron attended Riedinger Middle School, and while football was his favorite sport, his bedroom walls were owned by Michael Jordan. There were pictures, posters and Nike advertisements about Jordan and his shoes. Nearly every inch of his walls was covered with pictures at one point, most of them Jordan related. Those pictures were the last things he saw before closing his eyes at night, the first thing he saw when opening them in the morning.

So it was no shock when LeBron picked No. 23 to wear at St. Vincent-St. Mary High School. It wasn't an accident; it was a tribute to his favorite player. It also was a statement. He was aiming high, determined to be the best. Yes, he wanted to be another Michael Jordan, even if LeBron never stated it publicly.

"Actually, LeBron had to wear No. 32 when he first came to school because another player had 23," recalled Keith Dambrot, his first high school coach. "But the minute 23 became available, he grabbed it."

When LeBron was 16, he first met Jordan. LeBron was heading into his junior season. He had just been named the MVP of the prestigious ABCD Camp in July. He also had starred in several AAU tournaments with a high-powered team from Oakland, California which included future NBA players Leon Powe and Kendrick Perkins. Jordan had been retired from the Bulls, but was seriously considering a comeback with the Washington Wizards. He was holding private workouts in Chicago to get in shape. Jordan invited some pros, college players and a kid named LeBron James to come to Chicago and take part. It was also about this time that LeBron was becoming close to Antoine Walker, who was a star with the Boston Celtics at the time. Walker was from Chicago and was one of adidas shoes' top pitchmen. It is possible that Sonny Vaccaro, who knew Jordan well and also worked for adidas, introduced Walker to LeBron. Walker lived in Chicago in the off-season and was working out with Jordan at a local gym with other college players. And soon, LeBron had an invitation.

LeBron never played with Jordan then, but he

**THE LEBRON FILE**
LeBron is one of three players in NBA history to average at least 20 points, 5 rebounds and 5 assists in their rookie season. The others were Oscar Robertson and Michael Jordan.

**LeBron's desire to follow in Jordan's footsteps stopped at baseball, which his humorous batting practice session at Jacobs Field in 2003 showed.**

PLAIN DEALER PHOTOGRAPH | CHUCK CROW

did play with other pro and college players. At the time, LeBron was keeping a short diary for SLAM magazine, and wrote: "It was cool. I got to run with a lot of the other NBA guys and I talked to Jordan a bit … He really didn't give me any advice. He just told me to keep my head on straight."

In the summer of 2001, Jordan came to watch a game and LeBron had played very well. LeBron didn't realize Jordan was there until the game was nearly finished. He later told a reporter, "When he started walking over to me, I couldn't believe it was happening. It just didn't seem real. It was Michael Jordan. I was like 'Wow.' He just came over and stuck out his hand and said 'Hey there, young fella, you looked pretty good out there.' It was one of the most memorable things of my life up until that point."

A few months later, Jordan came to Cleveland as a member of the Washington Wizards. LeBron had courtside seats from Wes Wesley, a basketball business mover and shaker who is friends with everyone from Jordan to top NBA and college coaches to the shoe companies' executives. Wesley also befriends young stars, such as LeBron. He arranged for Jordan and LeBron to meet after that game. Later in the season, Jordan returned to Cleveland with the Wizards. He won the game on a last-second jumper, and LeBron was there again to see it.

When LeBron broke his wrist in Chicago at a summer basketball camp following his junior year, Jordan helped him get to see a hand specialist there. LeBron later returned to Chicago to have the cast removed by the same doctor recommended by Jordan.

A year later, after LeBron's senior season, he played in the Jordan Capital Classic in Washington, D.C. At this point a battle was being waged among Nike, adidas and Reebok, all bidding for an endorsement deal with LeBron. LeBron, Gloria and LeBron's new agent, Aaron Goodwin, came to

**THE LEBRON FILE**

LeBron is one of five players in NBA history to average more than 25 points, 7 rebounds and 7 assists in a season. The others were Oscar Robertson (six times), John Havlicek (twice), Larry Bird and Michael Jordan (once each). LeBron did it for the first time in just his second season, 2004–05.

Washington and had a meeting and private dinner with Jordan. It was assumed to be part Nike's recruitment of LeBron. Jordan also spoke to all the All-Stars invited to play at the game. LeBron was named the MVP of the game at the MCI Center (later renamed Verizon Center).

LeBron eventually did sign a shoe contract with Nike, and the numbers — a seven-year deal in the $100 million range — were only part of the reason. Reebok had also been bidding in the same neighborhood. An important factor was that Nike had developed the Jordan brand, and that a young LeBron had all those Nike posters of Jordan on his walls.

Not only does LeBron wear Jordan's No. 23 and wear the same shoes first endorsed by Jordan — there's the pregame ritual where LeBron comes to the press table, puts some resin on his hands, claps them together and then raises his arms above his head. It creates a white cloud of dust drifting down. Fans wait for it, television cameras focus on it, and it seems LeBron has made it his trademark. But Jordan also did it, and probably did it first. A young LeBron James also watched closely as Jordan did interviews, noticing how Jordan usually dressed extremely well when he was interviewed. Jordan stayed away from controversial answers, and usually made himself available for group media sessions, even if he didn't especially enjoy them. Jordan considered it part of his job, a good way to promote his sport, his team and yes, himself and his own products. He rarely was flustered by questions, rarely lashed out at media members. He usually was polite and patient. You can see many of these qualities in LeBron.

LeBron and Jordan never became especially close friends, though the two men do talk when they cross paths. But there is no doubt Jordan had an enormous impact on LeBron, on and off the court.

## MVP SEASON MOMENTS

Days after being named MVP, LeBron led the Cavs to a playoff series sweep of the Atlanta Hawks.

PLAIN DEALER PHOTOGRAPH | TRACY BOULIAN

## Chapter 7. "I Do My Work"

On the day that LeBron James received the 2009 MVP award, Barbara Wood sat in the gym at St. Vincent-St. Mary with tears streaming down her cheeks. The school librarian remembered how a young LeBron would walk into the library, and sit on her desk to talk. Sometimes they'd search his name on the Internet.

"During his sophomore year, he'd come into the library, stop at one of the computers and type 'LeBron' in Google. There were maybe 19 hits," said Wood. "I was flabbergasted. Back then Google wasn't what is it now, and if you were on there you had to have been written up somewhere. He was pretty proud of it. He knew how many results there would be and he was showing me. As the weeks went on, he kept coming back and checking. There'd be 30, 50, 100, 200, and it kept going from there." Just a few years later, a Google search on LeBron James' name would draw millions of results.

Woods remembered how she corrected his grammar: "There is no such thing as 'fiddy cent.' It's FIFTY CENTS ... with an 'S.' It's more than one cent."

At the MVP ceremony, he spoke with great poise, making his high school teachers proud.

"He didn't have it easy growing up," said Wood, "but he wanted a better life for himself and his family."

It is obvious that in his early life LeBron craved routine. It's why he bloomed as a student after moving in with the Walker family. It's why he may not have appreciated the discipline and firm hand of coach Keith Dambrot in his first two years of high school, but accepted it nevertheless. It's why he developed into one of the nation's best high school players by his 15th birthday.

**Life at St. Vincent-St. Mary was good for LeBron, but he had to follow the rules, including covering up his tattoos during games.**

It's also why the Catholic high school of St. Vincent-St. Mary near downtown Akron was a perfect place for LeBron to spend his high school years.

"He liked the order at St. V.," said Wood. "I think he would admit now that coming here was a good thing for him. He had stability. He had to follow the rules. He had to be somewhere on time. He had to keep his shirt tucked in."

There's more.

"He did his homework, always," said Wood. "He didn't have late assignments and he didn't have stuff missing. That was his work ethic in basketball and it was his work ethic in school. It carried over. I'm not saying he didn't mess around in some classes, I'm sure he did, but overall he always did his work. He would come into the LRC [the library] early in the mornings and after school before practices. This is when he did his work, so I know he was doing it. He was very conscious of what was expected of him and he always wanted to have it done."

PLAIN DEALER PHOTOGRAPH | CHRIS STEPHENS

Not only was LeBron the best player among the Shooting Stars, but he also had better grades than Willie McGee, Sian Cotton or Dru Joyce III. That says a lot about LeBron, because there was no one at home pushing him to make the honor roll, no one insisting that he do something extra in class. Yes, Gloria James wanted her son to do well in school and to stay out of trouble, but so did LeBron — and he wanted more. Just as something drove him to not only learn how to play basketball, but to study the history of the game as well, something inside LeBron made him want to be a solid student in school.

His favorite subject was English, and his favorite teacher was Beth Harmon.

"In his freshman year, I had this silly 'Romeo and Juliet' scrapbook project due on what turned out to be the Monday after the State Championship weekend," she said. "I was giving the basketball players an extension because I had all those freshmen at the same time. But on Thursday before they left for Columbus, right before the pep rally to send them off on the bus, LeBron stopped in and put the project on my desk. It wasn't sloppy and it was better than some of the other students who had a lot more time." Even then, LeBron wanted to please.

"He wasn't a perfect student, but he participated in class," said Harmon. "The atmosphere of 'family' at the school really appealed to him … He loved reading out loud. I had him in a class of 11 kids and there's always that person you need to get the ball rolling because there were some timid kids. He would always do that; he'd ask to read out loud and not all kids

are like that. He didn't like it if other kids were talking and I was talking. He would tell other kids to be quiet. Sometimes, he wanted to bring order."

Harmon said there were times when she did discipline him.

"I yelled at him in front of everybody and he sort of pouted and sat in his chair," she said. "I wasn't feeling well and the next day I had to get my appendix out. I was out of school for three weeks but when I came back he was so concerned. He didn't want me to get out of my chair or raise my voice. Once he helped calm down some students because I was getting upset. He did care about his teachers."

"It didn't surprise me that he could be successful academically," said Keith Dambrot. "I was surprised how little help he needed. He really did it on his own. He'd tell me, 'Coach, I'm not the best test-taker, but I do my work.' Not once did I have a discipline problem with him in school."

Early in his academic career, LeBron had a grade point average in the 2.8 range. It rose above 3.0 as a senior.

School administrator Patty Burdon said, "When LeBron was at the All-Star Games that kept him out of school, or on other trips, he's the one who said, 'I've got to get back to school; I've got a lot of assignments to make up.' He took pride in the fact that no one was going to do it for him. Most every other kid would have taken any bargain to get out of doing it."

LeBron enjoyed his budding fame and traveling the country and making news with his high school basketball team.

As Barbara Wood said, "He was proud of winning those awards, the Gatorade Player of the Year and USA Today Player of the Year. He was humble, but he was also excited. He would go around and remind people to come to the little ceremonies they were having after school when he got the awards. He liked to get those trophies. It wasn't a bragging thing; it was like he wanted some family to be there."

But he was also conflicted.

He knew that the University of Akron was making money from him when his team played at the 5,500-seat James A. Rhodes Arena on the college campus rather than their own small, 1,200-seat high school gym. He knew adults were selling his autograph on eBay for hundreds of dollars. He knew promoters were cashing in on his name when his team played in tournaments across the country.

"There would be times that some of our fans and boosters wanted private pregame meetings with LeBron," said Burdon. "There was one night where I saw them all go back there when he was supposed to be getting ready for the game. So I went back there and said 'LeBron, you are wanted in the locker room.' He looked at me and said 'Thanks,

**LeBron was suspended for two games for accepting free jerseys, making him an uneasy and unhappy cheerleader.**

Mrs. B.' He was trying to salvage what he had left of a high school experience while dealing with the pressure of being a pro."

"It was an adult-driven four years and that is something he resented," said Wood. "He never really got over that. He wanted all those games to be in the high school gym. He and I sat down before his senior year and composed a letter to the athletic director and the board of directors asking if he could have at least four games in the St. V. gym his senior year. We ended up getting two, including senior night. That was so important to him. The floor at the University of Akron was not student friendly and our students had to sit at the top and the parents and more expensive seats were on the floor. On senior night [the last home game for LeBron at the St. Vincent-St. Mary gym], Gloria wasn't there when it was time to be introduced. We didn't know where she was. It turned out she was handling a situation where LeBron had hit someone's car with his Hummer. None of us knew that. She was not trying to make a big deal of it. So all five seniors escorted him out. That turned out to be a real high point for him, getting to play at home for his senior night."

The library with Wood, and Harmon's English classroom became sanctuaries for LeBron, especially in his final two years of high school when he became a national celebrity.

"I had him as a freshman and sophomore; he was a solid 'B' student," Harmon said. "He was a pleasure to have in class, punctual and polite. As a senior, he'd come to my room and grab some of the candy on my desk. He helped me grade papers. I had a room attached to my classroom that we used for the yearbook work where it was usually quiet. He would come in there from time to time, even when I didn't have him in class. It was a quiet place to do some work and get away from everything."

Here was LeBron knowing that anywhere from $50 million to $100 million was coming his way within months, yet he enjoyed helping an English teacher grade papers in a quiet classroom during a free period.

Teacher Shawn-Paul Allison had LeBron as a sophomore for speech, and then as a junior and senior for English. Allison said he knew LeBron was a good basketball player, but had no idea of his national reputation until the middle of the student's junior year — probably when LeBron first appeared on the cover of Sports Illustrated.

**THE LEBRON FILE**
LeBron wears size 16 shoes, but Nike made molds of his feet and creates shoes to fit his feet exactly.

"I remember his senior year, he gave a speech in my English class," said Allison. "He talked about why it made sense for some people to jump straight from high school to the NBA. He had to do the research, and give real reasons. I worked with him a lot. I told him that he'd need these skills, and he has used them well."

If it was a course that LeBron liked, he went beyond the regular assignments.

"We were studying 'Macbeth' and he drew a picture with a pencil for extra course credit," said Allison. "For a few years, I had it on my classroom wall. But when he became famous, I took it down and put it in a bank vault."

LeBron was mostly a "B" student. Headmaster David Rathz said only once did he have to deal with LeBron on a discipline issue — for making noise in the hallway. More often, he remembered seeing LeBron in a geometry class, his long legs and knees up under the desk, his head down as he worked on a problem.

"As a senior, I called him in and said that I was supposed to tell him and all the other students they should aim for college," said Rathz. "But I smiled and said I wouldn't mention it again. He knew he was going to the NBA, but he still made the honor roll in his last grading period. He really wanted to do the right things."

LeBron did his fair share of goofing around in the halls and at lunch, but he was the one among his friends who would call them to order when necessary. He could sound like a crude young man right off the mean streets one moment, and a polite, private school–trained young adult a few minutes later.

By LeBron's senior season, many other things were competing with school for his attention. For example, he was being constantly wooed by shoe companies that wanted his endorsement and agents who wanted to represent him.

"His last few weeks of school were pressure filled," said Wood. "He was flying around after school to talk to the shoe companies. That was a problem — to keep him eligible to graduate because he was missing so much school. He always finished his assignments and he made sure he could get his stuff done. He never missed a day because he was sick. If he missed a day, it was because he had business to handle."

At that time, the NBA required prospective players to attend a Pre-Draft Camp with league-mandated physicals and interview sessions. LeBron was slotted to be at the camp in Chicago on Saturday, his graduation day, but he asked for and got an extension to Sunday so he could graduate with his class. Everyone waited in Chicago for him. LeBron made it clear that it was important for him to walk across the stage and receive the diploma with his class, especially with teammates Sian Cotton, Willie McGee, Romeo Travis and Dru Joyce III. They finished what they started out to do four years earlier — they made St. Vincent-St. Mary into a basketball powerhouse, and they stayed together and graduated together.

"LeBron had a great athletic body, but a lot of people have great bodies," said Burdon. She was more impressed with his drive to excel. "He got it from somewhere. This drive started long before the talk of the NBA started. He didn't know he was going to be a millionaire, but there was something in him from day one where he loves challenge. You have to be born with that. He could have gotten his diploma without going to graduation but he was proud of that, and he did."

LeBron stops by the school a few times each year. "Just him, not with his entourage," said Shawn-Paul Allison. He still wanders into the library and sits on Barbara Wood's desk. He also visits English

**LeBron is one of two players from St. Vincent-St. Mary whose jerseys were retired and who played in the NBA. The other was Jerome Lane.**

teacher Beth Harmon.

"I didn't have to push LeBron to do his school work, like I did some of the other guys," said Keith Dambrot. "He always did his work. When he was a senior and I was already coaching at Akron, I asked him why he still did his homework. I remember saying, 'LeBron, you really don't have to do anything in school.' He said, 'Coach, I have too much pride to go into a class where everybody else is doing their work and not have my work done.' LeBron really meant that. He has a lot of pride."

## Chapter 8. **Welcome to the NBA**

# A future MVP does his homework.

And for LeBron, homework didn't end with school. "I found that out right away," said Paul Silas, LeBron's first coach in the NBA. "LeBron knew that had I played in the league, that I had been on a championship team, that I was a good rebounder. He said he even saw some old video tape of me as a player."

They met in June 2003. Silas had not played in the NBA since 1980 — 23 years earlier. Yet the 18-year-old LeBron had made a point of researching his new coach, the man who would usher him into the NBA.

"I was shocked," said Silas. "Most kids his age coming into the NBA don't know much about history, and they don't care about it, either. They think basketball started with Michael Jordan. But LeBron knew about Oscar [Robertson], about Wilt [Chamberlain], about Doctor J [Julius Erving] and all the greats."

LeBron also knew something about the pretty good players, too — such as Silas, who averaged 9.9 points and 9.4 rebounds per game, and played on three NBA championship teams. He was also a two-time NBA All-Star.

Just as Keith Dambrot, a former Division I college coach, was ideal as LeBron's first high school coach because of his experience, Silas was a tremendous choice by General Manager Jim Paxson and Owner Gordon Gund to be the coach as LeBron first stepped onto a pro court.

For the Cavaliers, the blessing about the terrible 17-65 season in 2002–03 was that it gave them the best chance in the 2003 NBA lottery (along with Denver, another 17-65 team) at winning the rights to

**LeBron came to the Cavaliers with huge expectations, but his new teammates didn't make it easy on him.**

LeBron. It was less than a 1-in-4 shot, but on lottery night, the ball bounced the right way for the Cavs.

And they had LeBron.

But they also had LeBron coming to the worst team in the league. They had LeBron coming to a team that had been through four coaches in the previous five years. It was a team that had not had a winning record or made the playoffs in five years. It was a team that had stripped its roster of talent. It had also added more than a few immature and selfish players in the process of trying to lose as many games as possible in the 2002–03 season, so that Cavs could have the best shot in the 2003 draft at LeBron or Carmelo Anthony, their two top targets in the draft.

It might be useful to review some NBA history to put LeBron's rookie season into perspective.

As he entered the league, LeBron was compared to three players in terms of their ability to make an immediate impact: Larry Bird, Magic Johnson and Michael Jordan. They might be considered the blessed trinity of modern professional basketball, with Bird and Johnson entering the NBA in 1979, and Jordan arriving in 1984.

But there were significant differences between LeBron and the rest.

**Making LeBron the point guard as a rookie forced him to grow up faster than expected.**

Bird joined the 1979–80 Boston Celtics roster that included Cedric Maxwell, Nate Archibald, Dave Cowens, Pete Maravich, M.L. Carr, Rick Robey and Gerald Henderson. Archibald, Cowens and Maravich, though nearing the end of their careers, would eventually land in the Hall of Fame. Maxwell was a near All-Star caliber player. Carr, Robey and Henderson were all reliable veterans on a good team. They would finish with a 61-21 record and lose in the Eastern Conference Finals.

Magic Johnson was drafted by the Lakers, who had a 47-35 record the previous season. (The Lakers ended up with the top selection in the 1979 draft thanks to a trade with the Cavaliers.) John-

son's new Laker teammates included future Hall of Famer Kareem Abdul-Jabbar, along with Jim Chones, Jamaal Wilkes, Norm Nixon, Spencer Haywood, and Michael Cooper. It was a star-laden lineup that won the 1980 championship.

Jordan's rookie situation was closer to what LeBron encountered, but even he came to a Chicago team that was 27-55 with an experienced coach in Kevin Loughery. That Bulls team was bad, but did win 10 more games than the Cavs had the year before LeBron pulled on the wine and gold colors.

Among LeBron's first pro teammates, only one had been an All-Star — center Zydrunas Ilgauskas. It was a roster with many career underachievers and others of marginal ability. It had no veteran leadership and no discipline, after ending the previous season with an "interim" coach in Keith Smart.

While LeBron promised to "light up Cleveland like Las Vegas" on the day the Cavs secured his draft rights, to many in the NBA, the franchise had become a basketball Devil's Island. Few players wanted to go there, and even fewer who did play there wanted to stay. Paxson said he hated what he had done to the team, dumping decent players in favor of malcontents. But he knew the Cavs had to hit bottom before they ever could dream of moving up. And it worked, as all that losing did produce a winner in LeBron. Only now, LeBron was surrounded by all those losing players in a very depressed basketball culture. The year before, the Cavaliers featured Darius Miles and Ricky Davis on the cover of their media guide. Well, on media day, the annual preseason event at which each franchise shows off its new team to the news media, Miles "overslept" — though the press conference was held in the middle of the afternoon. Davis reportedly was "somewhere in Iowa," when he was supposed to be in Cleveland to meet the media and prepare for the opening of training camp the next day. Considering the baggage the team carried into that dismal 2002–03 season, you wonder how they managed to win 17 games. It was scary to think of bringing an 18-year-old number-one draft pick from a winning environment into a franchise in this state of disrepair.

**For long-suffering fans, just the act of drafting LeBron was reason to celebrate.**

Paxson knew he could make an immediate improvement by hiring the right coach. It came down to a decision between former New York Knicks coach Jeff Van Gundy and Paul Silas, who had been fired by the New Orleans Hornets after four consecutive winning seasons because there was a split in the ownership group. Paxson had been an All-Star guard. He had competed against Silas as a player, and knew the 6-foot-7, 230-pound forward was a man who used his wide load of a body to shove away opponents and create space under the boards to rebound. He had set picks that left some players wondering if they had smashed into a wall. Silas was not especially concerned about scoring, believing the game was won by rebounding, defending and playing together in a league where too many players consider "pass" a four-letter word that they didn't want to think about. While Silas' Hornet teams never won a title, they were generally considered overachievers, and a gritty, disciplined, unselfish reflection of their coach.

"We thought Paul, being a former player and having some success as a coach, could bring pres-

ence and stability to our team," recalled Paxson.

No one could look at the hulking Silas and doubt that he was an NBA player. He had a scowl that could cause a brick wall to shake, a stare that could shut up a player without the coach having to say a word. And when he needed to roar, he could come storming, his voice bellowing like an enraged bear convinced someone had just swiped his last meal. He once chased a Cavs player Ira Newble around the dressing room because Newble had complained about not playing enough in a loss at Atlanta. He was not afraid to bench some of his better players during a game if they failed to carry out assignments.

Silas knew he had four basic jobs that first season with the Cavs:

1. Create a sense of order and discipline so that LeBron would not be polluted by the me-first culture that swirls around so many pro teams. Battle the selfish players; demand that they respect the coaches and each other.

2. Make sure that LeBron makes the most out of his immense talents.

3. Put LeBron in the best situations to succeed

on the court — and off of it. Make sure he doesn't start going out with the "wrong" players and people after games.

4. Begin to push the team in the direction of winning.

The first time Silas saw LeBron play was at the McDonald's All-American game, a showcase of the nation's top high school players. At the time, Silas didn't know he'd be coaching LeBron. He just watched the game on television out of curiosity, aware that some of the players, including LeBron, were headed directly to the NBA. He would be seeing them soon.

Like most coaches, Silas loathed the McDonald's game. He considered it a pageant of strutting and showing off. Players just wanted to run and dunk. Defense was a rumor. There was always a disgusting lack of teamwork.

Yet Silas noticed that LeBron liked to pass, which made an immediate positive impression.

"Right away, it also was obvious LeBron's athleticism was off the charts," said Silas. "He could get to the basket at will. He could finish [make lay-ups] with either hand, a real plus because not many players even in the NBA can do that. His weakness was his outside shot, because he really didn't need it that much. He could get to the basket and score inside anytime he wanted — what high school kid was going to stop him?"

As an 18-year-old, LeBron was 6-foot-7¾ and weighed 242 pounds with seven percent body fat. It was as if God decided to create the perfect basketball body in one LeBron Raymone James of Akron, Ohio. Silas knew that the biggest battle for LeBron would not be on the court: it would be in practice, and on team flights and bus rides. It would be at the hotel after games. It would come from his new teammates.

The major influence on Silas was Red Auerbach, who won nine titles as coach of the Boston Celtics. He was the general manager of the franchise when Silas was traded to Boston in 1972. When Silas played for the Celtics, he used to spend hours talk-

ing to Auerbach. He would just come into his office and they would talk about the games and philosophies. Auerbach knew that Silas wanted to be a coach. He talked to Silas a lot about how to handle players.

At first, Silas was not sure of the best approach to coaching LeBron.

There had never been a player quite like LeBron coming into the league. Not even Jordan had the volcanic hype that surrounded LeBron playing for the team in his home town. Hard to remember now, but Jordan was the *third* pick in the 1984 draft, behind Hakeem Olajuwon and Sam Bowie. The consensus of most scouts was Jordan would be very, very good, maybe even great, but not that he was the best player in that draft. Aside from his pure athleticism and legs that seemed to act more like wings as he soared to the basket, perhaps Jordan's great asset was his background. He came from a middle-class, two-parent home in Wilmington, N.C. Jordan likes to tell the story of "being cut" from his high school basketball team, but that is only partially true. He was "cut" from the varsity as a sophomore, assigned to the junior varsity so he could play a lot and gain experience. His next stop was North Carolina, where he played three years for Hall of Fame coach Dean Smith in the rugged Atlantic Coast Conference. Smith had a share-the-ball offense strategy. He didn't run isolation plays for Jordan to take on opponents one-on-one, even after Jordan's medium range jumper gave the North Carolina Tar Heels the NCAA championship in 1982. Smith stressed team first.

Jordan's parents demanded respect and discipline from their son. It carried over to his willingness to submit some of his natural talent and his scoring average to blend into Smith's system that stressed ball movement, player movement and an offense that was not conducive to producing stars.

**LeBron's first Cavaliers' media day. Already the spotlight was on him.**

> **THE LEBRON FILE**
> LeBron was the youngest NBA player ever to be named Rookie of the Year, at age 19.

PLAIN DEALER PHOTOGRAPH | JOHN KUNTZ

**Darius Miles and Ricky Davis thought they'd be the stars, even with top draft pick LeBron James joining the team. Both were gone by the end of LeBron's rookie season.**

In NBA circles, scouts would joke, "Who is the only guy to hold Michael Jordan under 20 points a game? Dean Smith!" That's because Jordan averaged under 20 points in two of his three seasons coached by Smith. But that was good for Jordan. It taught him patience and delivered the message over and over that the basketball universe — or even his own team — does not whirl around him.

Then there was LeBron.

As the Cavs' front office and coaches looked at the kid from Akron, they saw an 18-year-old whose mother had a good heart but a somewhat troubled background. There was no father in the picture. There were some strong coaches in his background such as Dru Joyce II and Keith Dambrot from LeBron's days at St. Vincent-St. Mary. But that was high school. LeBron was on the cover of Sports Illustrated at the age of 17. By the end of LeBron's senior year, he had secured $100 million in endorsements from Nike and other corporations — all that before his first NBA dribble. Yes, he had good grades in high school. Yes, his coaches spoke highly of him. But

PLAIN DEALER PHOTOGRAPH | ROADELL HICKMAN

much [because of his fame], and he really did love the game. He was willing to learn. In terms of attitude, you could not have asked for more."

Their relationship began when LeBron came to the arena for a pre-draft workout. After the lottery, LeBron knew he was ticketed to Cleveland. The Cavs invited him to what was then called Gund Arena. Teams ask prospects to come to their facilities for a closer look before the draft. Some players may visit a dozen teams who could possibly select them. But this was LeBron's only visit, since he was the first pick. During that workout, it was only Silas and LeBron on the court. Silas put him through some shooting drills, Silas rebounding and throwing the ball back to LeBron so he could display his jumper from different spots on the court.

"I remember hearing an interview with Coach Silas right after he was hired," said Keith Dambrot, LeBron's first high school coach. "He mentioned that he had to see how LeBron would adjust to the game — mentally. I was thinking, 'Coach, you have no idea what kind of player you're getting — LeBron is a freak of nature mentally.' That's because as good as LeBron is physically, he's even better mentally. He has unbelievable knowledge of the game, and instincts for the game. He would throw balls behind his head because he *knew* where a teammate was. He didn't have to see the guy. He knew where every kid on every play was supposed to be on the court. When he played football one year, he was the scout team quarterback in practice, running the offense for the team that his team would play that week — because LeBron could learn their offense in football so fast. When it comes to this stuff, he's just a genius."

Silas soon learned that. He established a special relationship with LeBron, trying to do for the rookie what Auerbach did for Silas.

Silas knew there would be envy.

"My problem was never LeBron," said Silas. "It was some of the other guys on the team. During one of our first practices I noticed that, when we broke down to practice free throws at all the different baskets, no one was shooting with LeBron. Some of the guys barely talked to him."

Rookie hazing was a part of the NBA. On the

at 18, how mature are any of us? Then put $100 million into the equation, along with a public that had anointed him "King James." How often had anyone actually told LeBron "No," during his last two years of high school? No other player had ever entered the NBA with such lucrative endorsements or outrageous expectations as LeBron.

Everything was in place for him to be a spoiled basketball brat, a nightmare to coaches and the front office who are supposed to be his bosses. And how would he deal with failure and losing, which were destined to come during his first pro season?

"The first time I met him, LeBron was wise beyond his years," said Silas. "He had already seen so

Cavaliers, first-year players sometimes had to stop at a store and buy doughnuts for some veterans. Other older players could be a bit distant from rookies. There was some tradition of this in the league. Boston Celtic great Bill Russell refused to call first-year players by their names — they all were just "Rook" to Russell, only earning a name if they remained on the team for a second season. As an older player, Michael Jordan sometimes called rookies by their college name — "Hey, Vanderbilt…"

Silas knew LeBron had to endure some of this, but what he sensed that day at practice was deeper, meaner. He saw that some players barely spoke to LeBron on the bus or at practice.

"He didn't go out much with many of those guys," said Silas. "I know there were times when he felt lonely. He also was only 18, and couldn't go to some of the clubs that these guys liked. We had our security man, Marvin Cross, spend time with LeBron. What really bothered me is some of these players who never did a thing in the league were making it hard on LeBron."

Silas sensed they were feeling threatened by LeBron. They had little interest in helping LeBron assimilate into the pro game. This angered Silas, because the bottom line in the NBA is winning, and LeBron James at his best could take a losing team and turn it into a winner.

Making this even worse for LeBron is that he had played with the same core group of players since the fifth grade. Their journey began with the Shooting Stars on the summer courts of Akron AAU basketball.

Think about the loyalty and trust built up over those eight years. Think about LeBron's longing to fit in — as he did with the Walker family, and under the disciplined teachers at that private Catholic high school. Think about LeBron's desire for a stable family situation, and how the players and coaches from those Shooting Stars filled that huge, lonely hole in his heart. Then think about coming to the Cavs,

some of them mercenary basketball vagabonds who floated from team to team, not feeling connected to anything but their scoring average and their paychecks. Being with the Cavs was the first time that LeBron really felt on his own in a basketball setting.

"To make it even harder for LeBron, I had no point guard," said Silas. "I talked to LeBron about this, and he said he'd play the position. I'm telling you, he was special right from the start. He learned my offense faster than any of the other players. He is unselfish on the court. I knew it was a lot to ask, but I had gotten to know LeBron and believed he could handle it."

**THE LEBRON FILE**
LeBron is one of two players in NBA history to win the Player of the Month Award four times in one season. He did it in the 2008–09 season. Kevin Garnett did it in the 2003–04 season. Both won the MVP Award.

This would be like a football coach taking a rookie running back and asking him to play quarterback. Yes, both positions are on offense, and both are in the backfield, but the demands of the two jobs are much different. Or in baseball, it would be like asking a first baseman to catch. Yes, both jobs required the player to catch the ball, but the catcher also had to be responsible for choosing what pitches the pitcher throws — along with squatting down during the game and seeing it from a completely different angle than he did at first base.

LeBron was a small forward, a position that stressed shooting and scoring over passing. Yes, he was an excellent passer, but he had never played in the backcourt with the responsibility of not only taking care of his own game, but making sure all his teammates were in the right spots on the court — and that they saw the ball enough to get their shots. That's what Silas was asking, what LeBron immediately agreed to do. It's what won over many of his teammates, who knew how difficult it was for a rookie to make that adjustment. Soon, most began treating him as a real teammate. He no longer practiced free throws alone. He laughed with at least some of the players during bus trips. But as he approached his first regular-season game, there was more than a little trepidation. How would LeBron perform when it really mattered?

## MVP SEASON MOMENTS

LeBron and new teammate Mo Williams bonded
instantly in the 2008—09 season.

PLAIN DEALER PHOTOGRAPH | JOSHUA GUNTER

## Chapter 9. **Debut**

LeBron James sometimes insists he "never feels any pressure." Other times, he says he "welcomes" pressure. He has even said, "I don't believe in pressure." His former high school coach Keith Dambrot insists, "The bigger the stage, the better LeBron likes it."

No matter what LeBron claims, pressure is real and he felt it during that first pro season.

During the preseason of his rookie year, LeBron shot only 34 percent from the field. He was 4-of-14 in his first exhibition game in front of the home crowd in Cleveland, and in his first three preseason games, he averaged only 8.0 points.

Yet he was bold enough to say, "One day I hope [my jersey] hangs in the rafters."

Remember, this was said at the age of 18. When LeBron was struggling with a new team where many players didn't welcome him, where a veteran coach was asking him to play point guard, a position that was new to LeBron. He said it knowing he'd be in the same lineup as Ricky Davis and Darius Miles, two players who at this point in their careers cared only about their scoring averages and enjoying the glamorous lifestyle of the NBA. Both players were considered selfish and utterly uncoachable by many in the NBA. Even at 18, LeBron had to know this. Even at 18, LeBron realized the Cavs were not a talented pro team and that he was a marked man all over the league. Opposing veterans were thrilled when their coaches designed de-

**THE LEBRON FILE**

In his first home game as a Cavalier, LeBron scored only seven points in a loss to the Denver Nuggets. His friend, Carmelo Anthony, scored 14 points against him.

fenses to stop LeBron. Many in the media were already weary of the fanfare surrounding his arrival in the league, and would enjoy watching LeBron flounder — a way of putting the kid in his place, especially a kid who was talking about his jersey being retired before his first regular-season game.

In his first nationally televised game against the Lakers at Staples Center — we are talking about a *nationally televised exhibition game* — LeBron shot only 4-of-17 and looked lost. He wasn't sure when to shoot, when to pass, or even how to adjust to the 24-second clock. Remember that he came right from high school, where there was no shot clock. He also came from a great high school team with close friends who knew where LeBron wanted the ball — and he knew how to play so that he'd accent their strengths. He seldom seemed to have a shaky second in high school, but he ap-

**The media constantly swarms around LeBron throughout the season.**

As a rookie, there was intense interest in whether LeBron could live up to the hype — and his huge new shoe contract.

peared a bit rattled during this exhibition game. After watching LeBron shoot that rim-bending 4-of-17, an Associated Press writer who flew from New York to Los Angeles for the game noticed LeBron didn't do much pregame shooting. He wrote a story claiming the "H.Y.P.E." surrounding LeBron stood for "Hey You Practice Enough?" The story ran on the front sports page of the Bakersfield Californian the next day when the Cavs arrived in that town for another exhibition game. LeBron rarely reacts to anything negative written or reported about him now, and that also was the case dating back to high school. But this story did upset him, because it questioned his work ethic. He considered it an attack on his character and a cheap shot. That night in Bakersfield, LeBron played much better. In previous preseason games, LeBron had been playing sometimes at point guard and sometimes at his natural spot, small forward. But in Bakersfield, Silas put LeBron at the point — full time. His game began to show some flow.

Over and over, Silas kept saying, "The expectations are way, way too high. LeBron has the potential to be great, but it will take a while."

Privately, Silas thought LeBron could average 20 points as a rookie, but he didn't know if the 18-year-old could do that as a point guard. Silas also was concerned about asking LeBron to switch positions. He worried about the impact that Ricky Davis and some of the other veterans would have on LeBron.

No one — except perhaps LeBron — ever expected what he'd do in his first regular-season weekend.

The team had a crazy travel schedule. They played three preseason games on the West Coast, two in L.A. A few days later they were in St. John's, Newfoundland (a game cancelled during warm-ups because the ice under the court melted and the surface became too slippery to play on safely). Then came a three-hour flight from Eastern Canada to Cleveland. The Cavaliers were home briefly for one practice and a luncheon with season ticket holders. Then it was back to leaving on a jet plane for the West Coast again, for the season opener in Sacramento. They practiced on the Sacramento

Kings' home court at ARCO Arena the day before the opener. LeBron said he actually felt comfortable in this venue because he'd taped a Nike commercial at ARCO Arena with several of his teammates before the start of the season. Nike wanted to run the spot during the first day of televised games, and wanted it to be featured on the Kings' floor where LeBron would make his regular-season debut. It focused on how LeBron was laughing off all the attention paid to that game.

About 300 media members attended that first game, more than had been there for the Kings' final home game the previous season — and that was in the playoffs. More media coverage for a season opener between two middle-market teams in Sacramento and Cleveland than a significant playoff game. At the conclusion of the morning pregame shoot-around, a massive media crowd surrounded LeBron as he sat courtside. He had to ask people to move so that he could take off his shoes and put on his slippers to board the bus to get back to the hotel. The locker room at ARCO was too small to hold all of the media attendees, so LeBron had to hold his press conference outside of the locker room in a hallway.

The pregame was long because the earlier televised game had run into overtime. The TV network, TNT, insisted the Cavs and Kings wait for the conclusion of the opening nationally televised game. The network wanted a huge audience for LeBron's first seconds on the court. Nike and Coke, his main sponsors, had purchased large advertising blocks, and they wanted their commercials shown in the first half of LeBron's first game.

Watching from the stands were several sports celebrities who had traveled to the game, including Reggie Jackson, Terrell Owens and Dusty Baker.

As LeBron waited at the scorer's table for the game to finally begin, he was surrounded by cameras and photographers. He just sat there with his

**THE LEBRON FILE**

The most points LeBron scored in a game during his rookie season was 41, against the New Jersey Nets on March 27, 2004.

During his rookie season, LeBron scored 30 points or more 12 different times. He scored fewer than 10 points just six times.

legs swinging as he sat on top of the table while he was biting his nails. He appeared bored, rather than nervous, like a kid in a gym sitting on the sidelines awaiting a pickup game to end so he'd finally get his chance to play. While biting his nails may indeed have been an indication of some anxiety, LeBron said it was simply a habit he'd had since before high school. It was true: during high school games at St. Vincent-St. Mary you could have spotted LeBron sitting on the bench, nibbling on his nails, with his work done for the night as his team led by 40 points, another victory heading into the books.

In that game at ARCO, the Cavs started LeBron at point guard, with Ricky Davis at shooting guard, Darius Miles at small forward, Carlos Boozer at power forward and Zydrunas Ilgauskas at center. Boozer and Ilgauskas both eventually would become very productive players. Miles and Davis had had troubled careers before arriving in Cleveland, and not much changed for them later. Coming off the bench for the Cavs that night were Chris Mihm, J.R. Bremmer, Kevin Ollie and DeSaganga Diop. None of them would be considered starters in a winning pro team.

LeBron scored 12 points in the first quarter — defying the scouting reports that told the Kings' defense to let the rookie take jump shots. He swished his first four jumpers from the 15-to-20 foot range, three from the corner. He hadn't shot that well at any point in the preseason. At this early stage of his career, LeBron was a very streaky shooter. At times he could swish jump shots from nearly any spot on the court within 25 feet. Then the touch would be gone. He'd not only miss, he'd flip up some air balls in the general direction of the rim. He wasn't sure when or why the shooting touch would come, or why it would suddenly leave. It was like a bird flew in, landed on his shoulder, whispered something in his ear — perhaps, "Jump straight up as you shoot, don't fall away — and put plenty of arch on your shot." Early in that first game at Sacramento, he caught a pass in the corner. Seven-foot Kings center Brad Miller rushed out to block his shot, and LeBron lofted a high 20-footer over Miller's fingertips. Softly it went through the net.

LeBron also had two steals. One he threw down for a dunk that would become one of his season highlights. The other was the pass off to Ricky Davis for the dunk. On that play, he had a wide-open lane for an easy two points, but he waited as Davis came from behind, and at the last moment, he flipped the ball to Davis for a dunk.

"That's what point guards do," said LeBron, meaning a point guard doesn't worry about his own scoring; he sets up his teammates. Of course, LeBron had been a point guard only a few weeks. He finished with 25 points, nine assists, six rebounds, four steals and 12-of-20 shooting from the field.

The Sacramento Kings won, 106-92. But the team's front office acted as if LeBron were a new prince in town.

"This is the biggest regular-season game we've ever had here," said Joe Maloof, one of the owners of the Sacramento Kings. "There was a buzz around the city. It doesn't get better than this. This is great for the league. We need him. He's a breath of fresh air."

Remember, this was the *opposing* team's owner raving about LeBron. And remember, the Kings had been a very good team the previous season, reaching the 2003 Western Conference Finals. Even the Sacramento organization was being swept away in the tide of hype around LeBron.

"LeBron had so much to prove," said Silas. "The whole world was watching to see how he'd respond, and he came through with flying colors. At that point, I knew LeBron really had it."

"It" being the special quality that allows certain players to rise to an occasion. It's one thing for his high school coach Keith Dambrot to talk about how LeBron delivered even more when the stage

**At LeBron's first game in Sacramento, it often seemed the crowd was more interested in the visiting rookie than in the hometown Kings.**

PLAIN DEALER PHOTOGRAPH | MARVIN FONG

was bigger, the basketball stakes higher. It's different to do it at the age of 18 in the NBA.

"LeBron sees things on the court that no one else does," Silas said after that first game. "It's his vision. He sees passes no one else can even think about [attempting]."

One game never makes a season or a career, but it is fun to look at what Michael Jordan did in his first regular-season pro game: He had only 16 points, 5-of-16 shooting, six rebounds and five turnovers.

Of course, that changed quickly. Jordan had 37 points in his third pro game, 45 points in his eighth and scored at least 25 in 10 of his first 15 starts.

The Kings' style of play had helped LeBron. Like some other Western Conference teams, their main strategy was to out-run, out-shoot and out-score the opposition. But few athletes could match Le-Bron's long strides, his soaring steps as he vaulted to the rim. Basketball people knew it would be much harder for LeBron once the Cavs began to play the teams in the Eastern Conference. There, the tempo would be slower, the fast breaks fewer, the defenses more physical and more determined to guard the rim — rather than allow LeBron an open lane to the basket.

Nonetheless, it was the best start ever for a player coming directly to the NBA from high school. No one had ever had a debut like LeBron — not Kevin Garnett, not Moses Malone, Kobe Bryant, not anyone.

## MVP SEASON MOMENTS

Some of LeBron's greatest playoff moments have come against the Pistons, who the Cavs beat in 2009.

PLAIN DEALER PHOTOGRAPHS | JOHN KUNTZ

# Chapter 10. **Rookie of the Year**

Welcome to the NBA: LeBron James would open his rookie season with three games in four nights. After playing their season opener in Sacramento, the Cavaliers boarded a private jet and headed to the next stop — Phoenix, Ariz.

During the morning shoot-around in Phoenix, some of the players were already talking about where to party later that night. A morning shoot-around on the day of a game is primarily a mental exercise, the coaches having players walk through different strategies they plan to use during the game. It's a review session of previous practices, and a time when players are reminded of the different individual opponents they'd be matched up against that evening. Smart and dedicated players pay attention. But something else was brewing in the minds of more than a few Cavaliers. Because they planned to spend the night in Phoenix after the game, Ricky Davis was busy lining up a limo to take some of the players out to a club right from the arena after the game. LeBron was not invited out with the rest of the players. He was too young to get into the clubs anyway, but he also had few friends on the team at this point.

When it came time to play, most of the Cavs seemed to have their heads already at the post-game party. It was not much of a game, the final score being 95-86, and it didn't seem even that close. LeBron, though, had 21 points, 12 rebounds and eight assists. He nearly had a triple-double in his second game. While there were always Jordan comparisons with LeBron, this was more of a Magic Johnson–type game, a complete point-guard game. Coach Paul Silas was slightly concerned about LeBron having seven turnovers, but far more angry at the team's sloppy play and

**LeBron's rookie season turned out to be a difficult learning experience, as he dealt with mounting losses for the first time.**

the players' different agendas. The last thing Silas wanted was LeBron being dragged down by players who viewed the NBA as an entitlement program and a wonderful excuse to party.

The next stop was Portland, Ore., where LeBron and the Cavaliers would play the Trail Blazers, a team loaded with dysfunctional players. Some in the media called them "the Jail Blazers," because of all the legal problems being racked up by the players. Portland fans were disheartened by their team, but it was a sellout anyway — they had come to see LeBron.

This game was when the sad state of the Cavs really became clear to Silas — and to LeBron. Early in the game, LeBron passed twice to other players when Ricky Davis thought the ball should have gone to him. During a timeout, Davis screamed at Le-

Bron on the way to the bench. Most of the Portland players heard it. Davis wanted the ball and wanted the shots. He was obviously agitated by all the attention given LeBron. After all, Davis was supposed to be "The Man" on this team. He had averaged nearly 21 points for the Cavs in the previous season when LeBron was still in high school. So what if that team won only 17 games? Davis figured those Cavs would have been lucky to win seven without him. And all he heard that season while he was scoring those 20-some points a night was how the Cavs needed LeBron. Now that they had LeBron, it was even worse: the entire league seemed to be bowing down to the kid. Silas was far more worried about how to fit LeBron into the team — and blending the other players' talents with LeBron's. Instead, he should have been trying to fit LeBron's game with Davis', at least in the view of one Ricky Davis. In Phoenix, Davis had taken 25 shots, scoring 22 points — one more point than LeBron. He obviously wanted to outscore LeBron each night.

LeBron had never been a selfish player. In high school, he had been praised for his willingness to pass. He had averaged 31 points a game as a senior, and could have easily scored 50 a game if that had been his desire. He was stunned by the outrage from Davis. And as a result, LeBron turned timid. For the rest of the game, he didn't try to shoot much or drive to the basket. He just made basic passes, and finished with only eight points and six assists. After the game, Portland's Derek Anderson, who knew LeBron, stopped by the Cavs locker room and sent a note: "Keep your head up."

The Cavs lost to Portland, 104-85.

"The next morning, our team bus was supposed to leave the airport at 8:30 in the morning," recalled Cavaliers GM Jim Paxson. "We left at 8:38 because a few guys were late. Paul [Silas] went to the back of the bus, confronted the players, said he was not going to accept being late or accept losing. He was really upset. He also was exactly the coach we needed."

**The Cavaliers were still a long way from being a good team, but fans packed the then-named Gund Arena to see LeBron's first game.**

The Cavs returned to Cleveland for their home opener against Denver. In the stands were baseball player Ken Griffey Jr., rapper Jay-Z, several local professional athletes from other Cleveland teams and Nike CEO Phil Knight. The game would feature LeBron squaring off against Denver's young star, Carmelo Anthony, for the first time since their epic high school battle in 2002 when LeBron was a junior and Anthony a senior at Oak Hill Academy. In that game, the two players combined for 70 points.

LeBron had 36, Anthony, 34. The next season, Anthony attended Syracuse and led the Orangemen to an NCAA title. LeBron returned to St. Vincent-St. Mary, and led that team to a No. 1 national ranking (in USA Today). In the 2003 NBA draft, LeBron was the top pick, Anthony, the No. 3 selection.

This was yet another nationally televised game. The network was hyping it as the start of a new rivalry, comparing Anthony vs. LeBron to Larry Bird vs. Magic Johnson. In true NBA and network televi-sion fashion, the comparison was overblown. Johnson and Bird met in the NCAA championship game, and in the NBA they joined storied franchises — Bird with Boston, Johnson with the Lakers. LeBron and Anthony met in a regular-season high school tournament and were now playing for two dismal teams that were a combined 34-130 the prior season. But facts would not stand in the way of a network seeking ratings.

Before the season opened, Spike Lee, the actor/

director and self-appointed basketball expert, told the Associated Press this about LeBron as his rookie season began: "He has to perform. There's a lot of pressure on the young man. People aren't going to use the excuse that he's only 18. The reason why people forget is he's so mature ... You don't realize how big he is until you see him in person. His body is much more mature than the average 18-year-old's. What I think people will be impressed with is his basketball I.Q. The man is astute."

But LeBron was still 18. He was still new to the NBA. He was still a rookie, and still stinging from 3-of-12 shooting and being yelled at by Davis in Portland. It had been his first bad pro game, and he was having trouble shaking it.

His jump shot had been his best friend in Sacramento and Phoenix, but it got lost on the trip to Portland. It remained gone as LeBron stepped on the floor for his first regular-season home game. LeBron never talked about it, but the clash with Davis seemed to be weighing him down. Early in the game, he took a few shots that missed terribly, one an air ball about five feet short of the rim. He ended up with seven points on 3-of-11 shooting. His field goals were two dunks and a lay-up. Anthony had 14 points.

The Cavs were 0-4, and they had problems.

"What I was asking LeBron to do [change his position from small forward to point guard] is something you'd ask a five-year vet to do," said Silas. "I didn't want to put him in this position, but I had no other choice. He never complained. He listened. He learned the plays. He kept saying he just wanted to win."

LeBron tried to make life easy for the veteran coach, when it could have been a nightmare. LeBron could have gone to the front office and said, "They are playing me out of position." He could have gone to the press and knocked Silas because he had to play point guard, or ripped Davis for being selfish. He could have tried to divide the team by talking behind the backs of Davis and others to the players who did want to play team basketball. When LeBron could have acted like a spoiled 18-year-old, he trusted his coach. He also

**LeBron was a star from the start, leading the Cavs in scoring and setting numerous rookie records.**

listened to his coach. Silas told James, "Just play your game. If you have a shot, take it. If you can go to the basket, then drive to the basket. Don't worry about what anyone else says."

LeBron scored 23 points in his next game. But the Cavs lost to Indiana, making their record 0-5. LeBron had never lost five games in a row in his life, not even in summer basketball or peewee football.

A few weeks later, Davis ignored a play called by Silas during a timeout of a game. Davis wasn't the first option for a shot, but he didn't look to any teammate — just shot the ball himself, and missed. A week later Davis was again not following the game plan, and Silas benched him for the entire fourth quarter in Atlanta. Within days, Silas kicked Davis out of practice and refused to let him fly with the team down to New Orleans for a game. He suspended Davis for a game. He had a screaming match with Ira Newble in the dressing room in front of the media after a loss in Atlanta.

> **THE LEBRON FILE**
> LeBron has started every game he has played in his career except one, in 2007, when he was returning after missing five games because of a hand injury.

What does all this mess have to do with LeBron eventually becoming an MVP? It showed him the dark side of the NBA, a fast, painful lesson of what tears up and sinks teams. He was not with the Shooting Stars any more, not with his friends since the fifth grade who always could put their egos aside and play unselfish basketball when it meant the most — even if they were having some problems in their personal lives. LeBron was realizing that Dru Joyce III, Romeo Travis, Sian Cotton, Willie McGee, and his other St. Vincent-St. Mary teammates were far more mature than some of these men in the NBA. While he never publicly said it, there were times when LeBron was a little envious of Joyce III and Travis, who were freshmen on the University of Akron basketball team where Keith Dambrot was an assistant coach.

"I told Pax [Jim Paxson] that we had to get some of these guys out here," said Silas. "We needed to do it for LeBron, and also so I could get some discipline on this team."

LeBron had developed one friendship on the Cavs. It was with Darius Miles, who seemed shellshocked ever since being traded to the Cavs in the summer of 2002 from the Los Angeles Clippers.

He didn't like Cleveland, didn't like Silas screaming at him and was frustrated by the fact that his own career had stalled. Miles was the product of the summer AAU system, a physically gifted 6-foot-9 forward who had been selected No. 3 pick in the 2000 draft by the Los Angeles Clippers. In many ways, Miles had the same raw physical gifts as LeBron. But he lacked LeBron's discipline or willingness to work on the parts of his game that were the weakest. Because he could run, jump and dunk with the best in the NBA, Miles figured that was enough. He also came into about $20 million at the age of 18 when you added up his shoe deal and first NBA contract. That didn't exactly inspire Miles to put in extra hours at the gym after practice to work on his very suspect jumper. Nor did he have any great desire to improve his ball-handling, which was very erratic. While he was capable of driving to the rim and drawing fouls, he was about a 59 percent free-throw shooter — well below the NBA average of 74 percent. That never seemed to worry him, either. In many ways, Miles became the epitome of the pitfalls that could cause a teenager going straight from high school to the NBA and fail to even approach his potential. LeBron could have fallen into the same trap — floating through the league, averaging 10 to 15 points a season, playing primarily on bad teams and not being upset by any of it because the hefty paychecks ($4 million in 2003–04) kept coming. But that wasn't LeBron.

In fact, LeBron reached out to Miles, who LeBron thought could be painfully shy at this stage of his career. Just as LeBron didn't feel comfortable with many of his older teammates, neither did Miles — who was only 22 with the Cavs at the start of the 2003–04 season. The two played video games together. LeBron especially liked the Madden 2004 National Football League game, where he coached the Cleveland Browns and said he alternated Tim Couch and Kelly Holcomb at quarterback.

The Cavs started with a 6-19 record, Silas ago-

nizing about LeBron at the point, about Davis shooting constantly, about Miles playing with about as much enthusiasm as a man headed for a colonoscopy. LeBron was the NBA's Eastern Conference Rookie of the Month for November — as he would be every month that first season. At practice one morning in Indianapolis, Silas saw center Chris Mihm and Davis joking about how NFL player Joe Horn pulled out a cell phone and pretended to make a call after catching a touchdown pass. The coach watched Davis and Mihm as they talked about hiding a cell phone in the pad under a basket at the arena. They were joking, but Silas was livid. He told General Manager Jim Paxson that some of these guys had to go. Paxson had been working on some trades, and this pushed him harder. Within a day, Davis, Mihm and Michael Stewart were shipped to Boston for Eric Williams and Tony Battie. Neither of the new Cavaliers were stars, but both were hard-working veterans who understood what it meant to play in the NBA. They respected coaches and teammates, which is exactly what the Cavs wanted modeled for LeBron.

A month later, on January 21, 2004, Miles was traded to Portland for point guard Jeff McInnis. Paxson was worried that LeBron would be upset by the deal of his best friend on the team, and he wanted LeBron to know of it before the trade was announced. He found LeBron playing a video game, and told him that Miles had been traded for McInnis. According to Paxson, LeBron nodded and said, "We need a point guard." Then he want back to playing his game.

As a point guard, LeBron was scoring 20 points a game, but also was near the league lead in turnovers. Silas moved LeBron to the shooting guard spot formerly occupied by Davis, a position where he played on the wing much as he did in high school. McInnis ran the offense. The Cavs suddenly became a solid team.

The Cavs finished 35-47 — not great, but it was their best record in six seasons, more than doubling their victory total of 17 the previous season. LeBron was overwhelmingly named the Rookie of the Year. He became the youngest player in NBA

history to score 40 points in a game, 1,000 points in a season. He averaged 20.9 points, 5.9 assists and 5.5 rebounds — only the third rookie in NBA history to average at least 20 points, five rebounds and five assists in the same season. The others? How about being mentioned in the same sentence with Michael Jordan and Oscar Robertson, two Hall of Famers who held that distinction before LeBron achieved it?

LeBron was not named to the All-Star team, partly because he had a rash of early season turnovers as a point guard and partly because the Cavs were 20-33 at the All-Star break. He was invited to the Slam Dunk contest, but declined, much to the delight of the front office and coaches. LeBron was tired and feared an injury while dunking over and over in a contest. The Cavs thought the decision showed enormous maturity, because Nike and the NBA were pressuring LeBron to take part. Nike thought it was a good way to sell more LeBron James model shoes. The NBA knew that Le-

**As he accepted the Rookie of the Year award, LeBron and coach Paul Silas knew there were good things ahead for the young star.**

Bron doing anything increased television ratings. But LeBron said, "I look at myself as a basketball player, not a dunker. I don't want my stage to be the dunk contest." He turned down that same invitation in each of his first six seasons.

Cavs broadcaster Joe Tait said one of Silas' main concerns about his rookie was "that LeBron would get bored. He was so smart that he'd pick up Paul's plays right away. Then Paul would have to make the other guys practice it over and over. LeBron had to be patient. He already knew what to do."

The Cavaliers' attendance leaped from 11,497 per game before LeBron to 18,288 after. They had 18 sellouts of 20,562, second-highest in team history. LeBron had 13 games of at least 30 points. He dropped 41 points and delivered 13 assists against the new Jersey Nets. He didn't turn 19 until December 30, 2003. He also had a real exposure to the NBA as the Cavs shuffled through 21 differ-

ent players, attempting to find a dozen who wanted to play with LeBron, listen to Silas, and display some serious professionalism. Power forward Carlos Boozer would later grow into a star playing with LeBron. Veteran center Zydrunas Ilgauskas gained a real appreciation for LeBron.

"LeBron had a tremendous rookie season," recalled Silas. "There were times when I had to get on him to shoot more and to be more assertive — to talk to his teammates during the game. He was doing that by the end of the season. When LeBron came back for his second season with me, he already knew all the plays in our book — not just for himself, but where *every* player should be on *every* play. Very few guys do that kind of homework, to take the time to teach themselves all that, but LeBron is different. It's why I knew that one day he'd win an MVP award and that he'd become one of the greatest to ever play the game."

# Chapter 11. **All-Star**

When LeBron James made his first All-Star team, he had a runny nose, a bit of a headache thanks to a sinus problem, and a cold. He also was feeling drained as he sat in Denver's Pepsi Center, munching a giant turkey sandwich about an hour before he'd play for the Eastern Conference All-Stars. The date was February 20, 2005. LeBron was in his second season, and he thought this should have been his second All-Star game.

Instead, it was his first.

For all the awards and distinctions of his 2003–2004 rookie season, where he averaged 20 points, he was not voted on to the All-Star team as a starter by the fans, nor selected by the coaches. LeBron believed he belonged in that game. Great players often look for slights, real or perceived, as motivation. So often, athletes say, "They don't respect me."

For LeBron, not making that first All-Star team indicated a lack of respect.

In fact, he pouted, saying he wouldn't even accept a spot as an injury replacement. "I'm an only child, I don't come second," LeBron said at the time.

By the middle of his second season, there was no doubt — LeBron was among the NBA's elite players. And he wasn't even old enough to consume some of the drinks at the various All-Star parties, as LeBron was still only 20 years old.

The Cavs entered the 2005 All-Star week-end having played back-to-back games. It began on a Wednesday in Cleveland with a 111-89 victory over Atlanta, LeBron tossing in 28 points in 37 minutes and having the uneasy sense that he was getting sick. After that game, the team was ushered onto its private jet, and arrived in Minneapolis early Thursday morning for a nationally televised game with the Timberwolves. Although the Cavs lost 94-88, LeBron racked up 26 points, eight assists and seven rebounds. But early in the fourth quarter, he was helped to the locker room. He was sick to his stomach, his knees wobbly, his head dizzy. He had a severe case of the flu. He was given some fluids in the locker room and returned to the game with four minutes to play. He fell to his knees in the huddle during a timeout. Through it all, he still played 41 of 48 minutes. After the game he didn't even speak with the media, rare for him. Instead, he covered his head in a hot towel to help clear out his blocked sinuses. His head was pounding, pounding, pounding. His nose was running, running, running.

**THE LEBRON FILE**
LeBron was the youngest NBA player to be voted in as an All-Star Game MVP, at 21 years, 55 days old in 2005. Kobe Bryant had previously been the youngest player.

**LeBron stole the show at the 2006 All-Star Game in Houston, winning the MVP Award.**

GETTY IMAGES | NATHANIEL S. BUTLER

His body was aching, aching, aching — not exactly how he wanted to feel entering his first All-Star game. He took a private jet late that Thursday night from Minnesota to Denver. The next morning, he was due for his scheduled half-hour session with the world media at the players' hotel downtown. Then that night he had to play in the Rookie-Sophomore game, which he was required to do by the NBA. He'd compete for the team composed of second-year players.

This would be his third game in three days in three different cities.

By Sunday's All-Star game — the fourth game in five days for LeBron — he was starting to feel better. The fans had voted him to the starting lineup, and he delivered 13 points, eight rebounds and six assists. While those stats seem impressive, late in the game, when things got close and the players from each side shifted from "highlight mode" into actually wanting to win, LeBron took a backseat. Often he gave up the ball to teammates Allen Iverson and Dwyane Wade, even when he was in position to score. It was as if he was purposely stepping back, not wanting to step on the toes — and egos — of the older stars. Iverson had no problem with a starring role and took several passes from LeBron, leading the East to a win to taking the game's MVP Award.

After the game, LeBron was asked about his unwillingness to shoot in crunch time.

"My time in these games will come," he said.

Yes it did, one year later at the 2006 All-Star Game in Houston. Now 21 and averaging 29 points in his third pro season, LeBron knew he was poised to make this league his own. Always respectful of the NBA's history and its established stars, LeBron felt accepted by the greats in that All-Star dressing room. They not only appreciated his immense talent, but his unselfishness

**THE LEBRON FILE**
LeBron was the youngest player in NBA history to score 2,000 points in a season, in 2004–05, when he was 21. Kobe Bryant had previously been the youngest.

LeBron was the youngest NBA player ever to score 30 points, 40 points and 50 points in a game.

on the court. They remember how he intentionally stayed out of the spotlight in his first All-Star Game. Furthermore, LeBron was an easy person to be around. Yes, he liked to tell jokes and talk, but he also knew that he was the youngest guy in the room — and young guys need to listen. They need to ask questions. They need to remember that the game didn't begin with them, and a lot of good people paid some heavy basketball dues so young men such as LeBron could reap the millions of dollars, the incredible media attention and the worldwide fame.

The NBA All-Star game usually is a made-for-TV event, sort of like "Entertainment Tonight" for the casual basketball fan who is drawn to celebrity and slam dunks. Now in his second All-Star Game, his second start, LeBron was more comfortable in that dressing room. LeBron came into the game not only as the starter, but also the leading scorer in the Eastern Conference. His Cavs were on the way to making the playoffs for the first time in his career under new coach Mike Brown. The team had revamped its roster from the season before and LeBron had been named the team's captain for the first time — quite an honor for a 21-year-old. In addition, LeBron had received more than 2.2 million All-Star votes, the most of any player from the East. For the first time it seemed fans worldwide were embracing his position in the game. He also was coming off two big games on national television, scoring 44 points in a win over the San Antonio Spurs and then scoring 43 points with 11 rebounds in a game in Boston.

LeBron was moving from star to superstar, from being a great young athlete to the kind of player who one season could become the best in the NBA. And many of the older All-Stars knew it. Because the game was in Houston, it was assumed that it would be an evening to showcase Rockets' stars Yao Ming and Tracy McGrady. They were voted in as West starters. McGrady did play well and looked to be headed to the MVP, with the West up by 21 points in the second half. But this is where LeBron showed just how far he'd come.

As the game entered the fourth quarter, LeBron grabbed the ball repeatedly and attacked. He scored 29 points and made a series of key baskets in the comeback including two big 3-pointers late. On the game's final possession, a play was set up for McGrady to win the game for the West, which was behind by two points. As McGrady dribbled, then skidded to a stop to take what looked to be a game-winning and storybook 3-pointer in front of his home fans, LeBron defended him, McGrady's shot banging off the rim. McGrady and the Houston fans screamed for a foul. There was no whistle from the officials. The East won and LeBron took home the MVP Award. It made him the youngest MVP ever, edging out Oscar Robertson who was a year older when he won it in 1961.

After that game, Detroit guard and Eastern Conference All-Star Chauncey Billups said of LeBron, "He has a chance maybe to be the best who ever laced them up." It was high praise from an old-school guard, using old-school jargon for a 21-year-old star who also played for Billups' division rivals. What impressed Billups was how LeBron stepped up and grabbed control on a team that was packed with more established stars.

LeBron returned to Cleveland with not just a sense of accomplishment, but a sense that he was so close to becoming perhaps the best player in the NBA. He had a huge second half in that 2005–06 season, leading the Cavs to a 21-12 record down the stretch to clinch the No. 4 seed in the playoffs. His scoring averaged surged to over 30 points a game, which set a Cavaliers team record. During an important stretch to determine

**THE LEBRON FILE**
LeBron was the youngest player to be awarded All-NBA honors in 2005, when he was 21.

On Jan. 21, 2005, LeBron got a standing ovation from the Utah Jazz fans when he scored 51 points in Salt Lake City. Newspapers questioned the fans' loyalty afterward.

playoff positioning, he scored 35 or more points in 10 consecutive games.

When the regular season ended, LeBron was voted onto the All-NBA First Team for the first time in his NBA career. In the voting for the regular-season MVP, LeBron was second to Phoenix Suns point guard Steve Nash. He was not ready to win the big honor yet, but the media who voted for the award were no doubt awakened by his performance among the other All-Stars in Houston and then impressed with his strong play to finish the season. It set the stage for LeBron's first playoff performance, which included several game-winning baskets against the Washington Wizards and a dogfight seven-game series loss to the Detroit Pistons.

LeBron defended his position as the top among the All-Stars the following year in Las Vegas. LeBron again was the East's top performer as he scored 28 points and had six rebounds and six assists in a duel with Kobe Bryant. The West ended up winning and Bryant took home that MVP honor, but it was clear that LeBron had become the leader of the East, not just on the court but off of it. He was the emotional leader on the bench, and played 32 minutes, the most of his All-Star career. The next winter, in 2008, he kept it going at the All-Star Game in New Orleans. He scored 27 points with eight rebounds, nine assists, two steals and two blocks, and made 12 of 22 shots. In another closely contested game, his play proved again to be the difference for the East as it was able to get the win and, for the second time, he claimed the MVP. He became the 11th player in history to win the honor twice, and the youngest to do so. Between 2005 and 2009, he was the best All-Star performer, and he currently holds the highest scoring average (23.4 points per game) in the All-Star Game's history.

All that before the age of 25.

# Chapter 12. **Media Savvy**

LeBron James created a national sports stir when he refused to shake hands and speak to the media after the Cleveland Cavaliers were eliminated by Orlando in the 2009 Eastern Conference Finals. He came across as pouting and spoiled.

But that behavior was unusual for LeBron. The real story is how few times he has made major media mistakes, which is remarkable when you consider that he has been in the public eye since the age of 15. That was when LeBron was a star freshman basketball player at Akron St. Vincent-St. Mary. It also was when he no idea that he'd become one of the most recognized people in the world. Or that he'd appear on virtually every major television network and every top-ranked show from "60 Minutes" to "The Late Show with David Letterman" to "Saturday Night Live" to "Oprah." It was when he was 15 that he loved to see his name in the local sports sections, when he saved pictures of himself that ran in area newspapers.

There were even times when he believed he was ignored by the media. At the end of his freshman season, LeBron was upset when he was not named to the Ohio All-State team despite St. Vincent-St. Mary's 25-0 record. Traditionally, the All-State teams are selected after the regular season by a panel of media members, and it was explained to LeBron that freshmen seldom receive such recognition. However, he still felt slighted. A few weeks later, he was named the MVP of the Division III state tournament after leading the team to the state title, yet he longed for more attention. He would soon get plenty.

It didn't take long for St. Vincent-St. Mary officials to realize that they had something exceptional in LeBron. More and more reporters wanted to interview the teenaged star. Before going to the state tournament his freshman year, Headmaster David Rathz asked local reporters to meet with the team to discuss how to talk to the media. Coach Keith Dambrot schooled LeBron about how to be patient and polite with reporters. In some of the summer basketball camps that LeBron attended, there were presentations on how to behave during interviews. Interviews with sports stars were shown. Then public relations and media experts explained the basics of how to present yourself to the media. They talked about making eye contact when someone asked a question, about taking a moment to think before answering.

LeBron also liked to do his own homework, and he studied Michael Jordan during interviews. He noticed how Jordan rarely became upset by any

**As quickly as LeBron matured into an NBA star, he also developed into a great pitchman.**

**At the 2007 NBA Finals in San Antonio, LeBron was the marquee attraction.**

question, and how the superstar was always well dressed and groomed before appearing in front of the cameras. By his senior season, LeBron started working with a Cleveland-based public relations specialist, Alexandra Boone, and that added to his confidence in front of reporters and cameras.

An important person to LeBron in this area was Patty Burdon, an administrator at St. Vincent-St. Mary who handles much of the school's public relations.

"I gave him the Dennis Rodman example," said Burdon. "He was a great basketball player and a great rebounder, but most people will just remember him wearing a wedding dress (as part of a promotion for a book). I told LeBron to keep that in mind. He didn't want to be remembered for something like that. If you make a mistake, it will follow you for a long time."

LeBron went from being a local sports hero to a national figure in his junior season when he appeared on the cover of Sports Illustrated. The magazine had labeled him, "The Chosen One." The story written by Grant Wahl quoted former NBA player and coach Danny Ainge about LeBron being the league's next superstar. Ainge insisted LeBron would have been the league's top pick had he been eligible for the draft as a 16-year-old high school junior.

"LeBron was like a little giddy kid when that story came out," recalled Burdon. "[The story] was the talk of the town."

It also was when the reality of being a celebrity became a part of LeBron's life.

"[After the Sports Illustrated story appeared] about 50 different copies came in the mail from all over the place that people wanted him to sign," said Barbara Wood. "He signed them for awhile. But then he came to my desk and looked on eBay and found people who were selling the signed covers.

PLAIN DEALER PHOTOGRAPH | JOHN KUNTZ

He would point to them and say 'That's not my signature, that's not mine.' Then he said he was done signing them. And I didn't blame him. It was such an eye-opener to him. He was like a kid who had his innocence taken away right there. I don't think he was the same after that."

LeBron stopped signing autographs for adults, believing they all were just using him to make profit. His personality began to take on a harder edge when in public, as he sensed people were out to use him. He sometimes was correct, but not on every occasion. In the process, he hurt some of the feelings of fans who simply wanted to wish him well and perhaps shake his hand. LeBron said in an interview with "60 Minutes" in 2008 that he didn't grasp the importance of being on the cover. He knew it was a big deal at the time, but still didn't know the impact it would make — the cover took him from a local to a national story.

Now it is common for high school games to appear on local television and also on the national cable outlets of the various ESPN channels. But it was still rare when LeBron made his first national television appearance in December of 2002 when the St. Vincent-St. Mary Fighting Irish faced prep powerhouse Oak Hill Academy.

"ESPN approached us about putting that Oak Hill game on the air," recalled Burdon. "Then I'm watching the pregame and [ESPN college basketball analyst] Jay Bilas is talking about how the school was exploiting the young man. That made us so angry because they approached us, it was their cameras. It didn't bother [LeBron] one bit. [Sportscasters] Dick Vitale and Bill Walton were in the locker room before the game."

LeBron led his team to a 64-45 rout. The game was played at the Cleveland State University Convocation Center in front of an estimated 13,000 fans, most of whom didn't realize was the pressure on LeBron that evening. He was a senior, heading into the NBA draft. Shoe companies were already bidding for his endorsement. Millions upon millions of dollars were on the line. Remember that poverty had been a part of LeBron's life. Not only was this a chance to increase his value in the eyes of the shoe companies, but to also make so much money before his first pro game that his family and anyone else he wanted to help could be set for life. A poor performance against the nation's top high school team in front of ESPN's cameras while Vitale and Walton supplied the commentary could have been a real setback to LeBron's dreams for his family. His mother, Gloria, was especially anxious that night.

"You could just see the pressure on Gloria's face," said Burdon. "She was a mother, and she was afraid for her son. What if we put him on national TV and [he] doesn't have a good game? All of this could go down the tubes. I know people were telling her that we [St. Vincent-St. Mary] were selling her son [by playing a national schedule and playing on ESPN]. Her mom genes really kicked in there (and Gloria James didn't like the idea of the national exposure). But everybody else wanted to go for it, especially LeBron. He was like, 'Bring 'em on.'"

Then the school began to back away from some of the offers.

"The next time they [ESPN] came to us that year, we told them no," said Burdon.

During LeBron's senior season, ESPN The Magazine published the first negative story on LeBron. Written by Tom Friend, the piece was highly critical of Gloria, and brought up her personal problems and hinted of shady dealings. People in the local media knew that Gloria James had had a lot of struggles in her life, but saw no reason to write about it. Why embarrass LeBron because of some poor decisions made by his mother? Despite all the hype, he still was a high school athlete and didn't even turn 18 until the middle of his senior basketball season.

Friend then followed up the story with interviews on various ESPN shows and continued to be

> **THE LEBRON FILE**
> In 2006, LeBron hosted ESPN's ESPY Awards. He also has won three personal ESPYs: the 2004 Best Breakthrough Athlete ESPY Award, the 2007 Best NBA Player ESPY Award, and the 2009 Best NBA Player ESPY Award.

negative about LeBron's mother, and the entire situation at St. Vincent-St. Mary. LeBron's view of the media started to change rapidly, and he began denying most interview requests.

"There were times when he would just pull his arm away and say he wasn't doing it," said Burdon. "He knew there were some things that were legitimate, and he got to the point where he knew dealing with the media became business. When the Letterman show called ... then Leno, Oprah, Regis and Kelly, we realized we had a monster here. When they would call I would try to be calm and act like we deal with this all the time and we were equipped [to handle it]. I had no clue what to say to these people. We were all kids at this point. We would take it to LeBron and see how he felt about them. Most of time he said 'No.'"

"He came in one morning at 6:30 a.m. and there was media all over the place," recalled Wood. "People were getting to the school at 6 a.m. to buy tickets to the big games at the ticket office. One of the television stations came into [the library] and wanted an interview. LeBron looked up at me, this big 6-foot-6 kid with these puppy-dog eyes, and he said, 'Do I have to do this interview?' I told him, 'Absolutely not.'"

During LeBron's senior year, the media was banned from the school during class time, and school officials helped LeBron guard himself from the media.

Many young stars in sports and show business have been turned into media-hating brats by experiences far less intense than those endured by LeBron during his high school years. But LeBron went on to develop and maintain solid relationships with the media when he joined the NBA.

He received the standard media training during the NBA Rookie Symposium. Despite all his media exposure, he was at one disadvantage coming into the NBA. Without the college experience, LeBron was not used to the regimented daily media grind that was waiting for him in the NBA. The league depends on promotion to sell tickets. Part of that is dealing with newspapers, radio and television stations in all of the league's markets.

Another part of the publicity machine is the NBA-sanctioned networks that broadcast the games. The players and coaches have to do their part to keep interest in the league by dealing with the media. Most of the players who come to the NBA from major colleges have had a taste of this. They are used to talking to reporters and doing interviews after practices, not just games. They experienced large media situations in controlled situations like the NCAA Tournament.

LeBron may have dealt with more media than any other high school basketball player in history. He was bothered in school. He was bothered when he was out on the street. At 18, he was already feel-

**LeBron has become at home on sets and in studios like this one, where he recorded radio ads.**

ing burned out by all the bright lights of the cameras and bored by most questions from reporters. The 15-year-old freshman who saved newspaper stories and photos of himself sometimes thought he could live just fine without the attention by the time he was 18.

But in 2003, the NBA needed LeBron to be a fresh face. LeBron went to his hometown Cavaliers, who had been last in the league in attendance. They hadn't been on national television in three seasons, and hadn't made the playoffs in five years. They were losing nearly a million dollars a month for al-

most two years before the lottery Ping-Pong balls bounced just right, and LeBron became the first draft pick of his hometown team. The Cavs knew LeBron could quickly revive the almost comatose financial condition of the franchise. The team showcased him in every possible venue. When LeBron came in for his predraft workout, even before he was a member of the team, there were about 100 media members on hand — all invited by the team. They watched him practice alone.

The day after he was drafted, an even larger media turnout showed up at the arena. They were joined by about everyone who worked for the Cavs and the arena so there would be a loud cheer when LeBron was introduced with his Cavs jersey. Later in the summer, the Cavs even invited the media to a recording studio in suburban Cleveland just to watch LeBron record some radio commercials for the upcoming season. The team wanted LeBron in the news as much as possible during the dead summer months — and they enjoyed more positive off-season positive headlines than at any time in the history of the franchise.

LeBron did it, but he was weary of the media before his rookie season even began. In an effort to appease the huge interest he generated in every town the Cavs played during his rookie season, LeBron would often meet with the media three times a day during game days. He would talk after shoot-around in the morning, then he would speak about an hour and a half before the game, and then a third time after the game.

Whenever the Cavs were on national television, which was a lot in the early part of the season, the various networks wanted a private interview that would often have to fit into that schedule. Virtually no player in the league has such demands and many of the stars talk just once on the day of a game.

"We [the Cavs] never had a player with the media demands on him like LeBron," said Joe Tait, the Cavs broadcaster for all but two years in the history of the franchise. "I watched him do the interviews, and it was like he'd been doing it all his life. I know it had to wear him out, but I never heard him complain about it."

However, LeBron was telling the public relations people that he was indeed getting tired of the three interviews a day. But he didn't always say no at the right times. During the preseason, Sports Illustrated wanted to do a photo shoot to feature LeBron on the cover for its NBA preview issue. It was a rare honor for a rookie, to be on the cover of Sports Illustrated. To shoot the cover, the mag-

> **THE LEBRON FILE**
> LeBron has been a guest star on several television shows, including "The Simpsons," "Entourage," "My Wife and Kids" and "SpongeBob SquarePants."

azine assigned Walter Iooss, one of the most respected photographers in the world. He had shot nearly 300 SI covers. Jack McCallum, who was the magazine's lead basketball writer at the time, came to town to do an interview. LeBron granted them a total of 30 minutes for the photo and the interview. When he was photographed for the cover of Sports Illustrated two years before, LeBron had allowed an entire morning for the shoot. He allowed the reporter, Grant Wahl, several days of access. This time, Iooss received about 20 minutes and created what was perhaps the most mundane of the dozens of magazine covers that have featured LeBron. On this cover, LeBron stares at the camera with a basketball in his hand, his uniform untucked. McCallum's story was equally bland. LeBron's media fatigue caused him to make a decision that gave a major national media outlet a negative impression of the 18-year-old star, a sense that he was spoiled.

Later that year, the Cavs were featured on national television on Christmas Day, playing in Orlando against the Magic. This was a big television ratings day for the NBA, which was in the second year of a new television deal with ESPN and ABC. The Cavs and Magic were playing on ESPN. After that game, ABC featured a game between the Lakers and Rockets with Shaquille O'Neal facing Yao Ming. ABC wanted to do an interview with LeBron right after the game — for its pregame show for the Lakers/Rockets game.

LeBron played one of his best games of that season with 34 points, but Tracy McGrady scored 40 as the Magic won in overtime. LeBron was frustrated by the loss, and the overtime sped up the TV timetable. ESPN's John Saunders came running from his courtside seat to a private room set up next to the Cavs locker room for the live interview. But LeBron refused. ABC was expecting him. A member of the Cavs media department was down on his knees in the locker room and spoke into LeBron's ear. He tried to explain how important it was to the NBA and ABC. LeBron declined several times.

There were a few times during the season where LeBron blew off previously scheduled interviews with national media outlets or television outlets. Despite talking with the media so often, those events hurt his reputation in that rookie season. His problem was figuring out who were the major media players, and who were the minor ones. He was 18 at the start of his rookie season. By his 19th birthday, he already had been interviewed more times than many NBA players are for their entire careers.

Over the next few years, LeBron found a routine with the media and his relationship with them changed for the better. He became much more accommodating, and learned to take care of all the major media outlets.

"He does more press conferences than any superstar that I've been around," said veteran Cavaliers television broadcaster Fred McLeod. "He does pregame and postgame interviews. He does an interview after nearly every practice. He looks the person asking the question right in the eye. You can see him thinking before he answers. I have been in the NBA for 27 years, and he handles the media as well as anyone I've seen."

The Cavs set up group press conferences for LeBron lasting about 10 minutes. Very rarely will LeBron do a one-on-one interview with a local writer or broadcaster.

Joe Tait does one radio interview a year with LeBron.

"He never turns me down," said Tait. "He has so many people pulling at him, I don't like to bother him."

Gloria James loves to listen to Joe Tait. Whenever she spots the burly Cavs broadcaster, she rushes to him and gives Tait a huge hug. Tait appreciates the fact that LeBron is "always on time" for planes and buses.

"We've had stars like Shawn Kemp who were late for everything," said Tait. "Drove me nuts. Le-

**THE LEBRON FILE**
LeBron has had his own flavor of Powerade, "FLAVA23.". He had his own flavor of Bubblicious gum, "LeBron's Lightning Lemonade," named after one of his favorite drinks.

Bron acts like one of the guys. He's pretty quiet on team planes, unless they get a card game going — and then he's telling everyone around him how much money he plans to win off the other guys."

Does he do that?

"I know he talks a good card game," said Tait. "Not sure how he plays."

That wisecracking card player is not something LeBron shows the public. He comes across as "an old soul," McLeod said. Maybe not old, exactly, but LeBron usually sounds and acts more like he's in his 40s than his 20s.

"I am amazed how he doesn't get bothered by even the dumbest questions," said McLeod. "He listens to what is being asked. It's like he is on the court — as good as he is physically, he's better mentally."

LeBron can frustrate some media people because he won't allow them to ask a question without everyone else at the game that day hearing it — no private time with the star.

"Everything is in a structured setting," said Jeff Phelps, a veteran Cleveland TV sportscaster who also hosts the Cavs pregame and postgame shows. "But you have to do it that way because so many people want to talk to him. He is extremely professional, always polite. He says something you can usually use on the air, even if he is careful what he says. He is very impressive."

Phelps covered some of LeBron's high school games for a Cleveland cable TV station.

"I still remember LeBron as a kid who liked being on TV," said Phelps. "Before one game, they gave out little fans with his face on them. He came to press row and gave us all one — he got a real kick out of that fan. I have watched him grow up not just as a person, but as a media personality. He cares about how he comes across in the media, which is not true of every player."

After his second year in the league, LeBron reworked his off-the-field management and hired a new agent. He also retained Keith Estabrook, a

New York-based publicist with experience in the entertainment industry, especially working with musicians. LeBron was creating his own marketing firm called LRMR with several friends. Estabrook worked with LRMR to expand LeBron's appeal to large national and international media outlets.

LeBron became a frequent guest on "The Late Show with David Letterman" on CBS.

"I saw him on Letterman and it was like he did the show every other week," said Tait. "He was completely relaxed. He smiled at the right times, cracked some jokes. It was like he was born to do this."

He appeared on the cover of GQ in a finely tailored suit. He was on the cover of Men's Fitness. He did lengthy interviews and photo sessions with the financial press, such as Forbes and The Wall Street Journal. In 2008, he became only the third man in 116 years to grace the cover of Vogue, a major fashion magazine. The others were actors Richard Gere and George Clooney. He appeared with supermodel Gisele Bundchen in a photo shot by famous photographer Annie Leibovitz. He allowed a lot longer than 20 minutes for that. It was like a small movie set in Akron with dressing rooms, space heaters and fans.

LeBron also agreed to appear on Oprah Winfrey's talk show. He brought along his mother and his longtime girlfriend and mother of his two children, Savannah Brinson.

On "60 Minutes," a show that specializes in investigative journalism and doesn't always focus on the positive side of its subjects, LeBron charmed normally hard-hitting reporter Steve Kroft by nonchalantly throwing in a 70-foot shot during an interview at his old high school gym. Rather than a series of hard questions and answers, that incredible shot became the most memorable part of the interview. That's because LeBron handled the questions so coolly — and you could see that Kroft immediately took a liking to the young star.

"LeBron learned fast that he can be the face of his team, the face of the league and even a global star by how he deals with the media," said Jeff Phelps. "He wants people to like him, and he knows that doing a good job with the media is a way to make that happen."

**LeBron launched the Nike Air Max LeBron VII shoe at the Ed Davis Community Center in Akron.**

PLAIN DEALER PHOTOGRAPH | LISA DEJONG

# Chapter 13. **Pitchman**

When most LeBron James fans think about their favorite player appearing in commercials, they remember "The LeBrons."

For good reason, it shows the MVP can act a bit. His evolution as an actor also reflects his growth as a leader on the court, becoming more vocal and confident over the years.

Granted, Denzel Washington was not about to lose any sleep about LeBron taking his roles, but for an athlete in his early 20s who was never trained in drama and had no show business background, the talent was clear. As they say in Hollywood, the camera likes LeBron. And just as important, LeBron loves being in front of the camera. He has the patience to do the same scene over and over, hour after hour, He has a magnetic smile, a terrific memory, a natural personality — much like Michael Jordan — that makes him very attractive to advertisers.

"The LeBrons" demonstrated as much.

It was LeBron's idea and played off one of his favorite movies as a child, "Coming to America," where star Eddie Murphy plays several different characters. In the spots, which ran for more than two years and became more creative along the way, LeBron played four different characters that we saw on the screen at the same time. The idea was to show other sides of his personality.

There was "Business LeBron," a slick talker who was modeled after a 1980s yuppie, complete with cell phone, immaculate three-piece suits and big hair.

There was "Wise LeBron," which called to mind Fred Sanford of "Sanford and Son." He wore a beard and lectured the others on how to play. He bragged about his exploits as a young man, once claiming to have a quadruple-double.

There was "Athlete LeBron," who was the Le-Bron that fans see on the court.

There was "Kid LeBron," which focused on the inner child LeBron still feels he is, complete with horseplay and pranks.

"It was a chance to show my personality; it wasn't really much acting," LeBron said. "They were very long shoots. It took forever to get into some of the makeup but I felt like it was a way for me to be genuine."

But it wasn't always like this for LeBron.

Right before the 2003 NBA draft lottery, LeBron signed a record-breaking $90 million contract with Nike. It was a stunning deal because LeBron was only 18, had yet to take a single shot as a pro — and Nike didn't even know where he would play. His former agent, Aaron Goodwin, deserves his own MVP award for pulling that off. Nike moved slowly with its teenaged prodigy, not knowing if he had any acting talent. LeBron didn't have a spoken line in his first three television commercials for Nike. The spots were slick, as many of Nike's have been through the years. It also used up millions of dollars and the designs of Portland, Ore., firm Wieden+Kennedy — which has become legendary for its creativity in Nike spots for many years.

In the first spot, which was filmed just before training camp in 2003 with several of his teammates in Sacramento, LeBron just stands on the court while other actors, such as Damon Wayans, and NBA greats comment on the pressure he was under as a rookie. It was played during LeBron's first game in Sacramento. All it showed LeBron doing was smiling and dribbling.

The second commercial was the first big-budget spot from Wieden+Kennedy. It featured the late comedian Bernie Mac, who played an energetic preacher on a basketball court that was fashioned into a church. It was a play off of LeBron's nickname as "The Chosen One" and showed him coming into the "church" and passing instead of shooting. In addition to Mac, it also had cameos from NBA greats Julius Erving and Jerry West.

The third Nike commercial was produced in LeBron's second season. It was an animated video game-type spot with LeBron performing kung fu and taking on Asian warriors and dragons with a basketball. It was banned in China because the government found it insulting to their national heritage. Considering that LeBron was trying to corner the Chinese market, it was a mistake. Nor did the spot do anything to reveal LeBron's personality. LeBron also was learning that he could do more in front of the camera, and he began pushing for better roles in the Nike spots where he is more than an almost cartoon-type character.

At the time he was also doing some commercials for Sprite as part of his deal with Coca-Cola. While he did get some speaking lines, one of the more memorable spots featured a crunching sound. In it, it appears that LeBron had snapped his neck, but it turns out he was only crushing an empty plastic Sprite bottle to scare his friends. In another spot, a puppet named "Miles Thirst" overshadowed him.

As LeBron entered his third season with the Cavs, he was named team captain. He was 20 years old, and his confidence was growing on the court — and off. He began to insist that Nike give him commercials with more speaking lines, more chances to be something other than a cardboard character. Nike agreed and created a new series of commercials. That series, "The LeBrons," required more acting talent of LeBron than is required of most athletes serving as commercial pitchmen. Suddenly, LeBron was being taken more seriously as a television performer

**The huge Nike billboard outside Quicken Loans Arena in Cleveland has been declared public art by the City of Cleveland.**

— at least compared to other superstar athletes. He was definitely not an embarrassment in front of the camera. He hosted the ESPY Awards and performed a big musical number to kick off the show. Later he became the first NBA player since Michael Jordan to host "Saturday Night Live." He also made cameos in several television shows including "My Wife and Kids" and "Entourage."

As he continued to draw comparisons to a young Michael Jordan on the court, he was also beginning to rival Jordan as a polished spokesman. Corporations liked how he had fans of all ages, races and political leanings — just like Jordan. Both athletes make people feel comfortable and inspire smiles when their commercials splash across the screen.

LeBron's other sponsors took notice of the new Nike commercials and started giving him more speaking roles and comedic roles. Coke used him in ads for Vitamin Water, which featured him as a defense attorney in a courtroom. State Farm showed him mocking a friend after his car was broken into without the proper insurance. That spot had him mocking Richard Paul, one of his close friends, and

PLAIN DEALER PHOTOGRAPH | THOMAS ONDREY

dancing with another, Randy Mims (both executives in LeBron's LRMR Management company). They were letting their hair down a little and having fun.

"At the end of the day, they know I'm going to make the right decision for myself and for my family and for the companies I'm with," LeBron told GQ. "I never just wanted an endorsement deal where they write me a check and say we need you here these nine days and you have to do what we say. I think I'm much bigger than that. My personality's much bigger than that, and I can help them out as much as they can help me out."

His commercials have improved over the years, according to advertising reviewers such as the Web site Great-Ads, which commented: "Even by the high standards of LeBron commercials, the new "Chalk" Nike Zoom LeBron VI ad is pretty entertaining. The black and white shoot gives it that added texture."

The spot featured LeBron and his ritual of throwing his white cloud of resin above his head to start a game at Quicken Loans Arena. Then it showed people from all walks of life doing the same, imitating LeBron.

"Before we even get to the director, we have these meetings in Oregon, where the campus is, and we

talk about certain ads that we want to do," LeBron told GQ. "I have just as much input as the guy who thought of the ad."

A commercial that showed particular depth from LeBron is one called "Nike After Six." The spot features LeBron and Nicole Scherzinger, part of the girl band The Pussycat Dolls. It was nearly five minutes long and shown only on the Internet. In it, LeBron wears an Afro hairstyle along with a 1970s "Super Fly" suit with wide lapels. He is indoors, with lighting turned down low, and a fire glowing in the fireplace, but even so he's wearing sunglasses. Scherzinger is decked out in a sexy black evening dress. It appears that he's about to give her a box with an engagement ring, and it turns out to be a new pair of LeBron's latest shoes.

The Web site Urban Daily rated LeBron's commercials. They gave a special mention to "After Six," but here's the list of the top five:

1.  State Farm Insurance: LeBron dancing in a parking garage
2.  State Farm Insurance: LeBron signs with the Cleveland Browns
3.  "ESPN Sportscenter": LeBron gets kicked out of a chair
4.  Vitamin Water: LeBron as an attorney
5.  Nike: "The LeBrons"

To date, LeBron has made about $130 million from different endorsements. LeBron takes all of this very seriously. He has long been interested in money. His former high school coach, Keith Dambrot, recalls an 18-year-old LeBron telling him, "Coach, I'm reading financial magazines now."

"Business LeBron" is a large part of his personality. He enjoys meeting successful business people. He struck up a friendship with Warren Buffett, considered perhaps the wisest investor in America. In the summer of 2009, he attended the Allen and Company Sun Valley media summit held each year in Sun Valley, Idaho. Cavaliers owner Dan Gilbert brought LeBron along. There, he had a chance to mingle with top executives such as Buffett, Barry Diller, Michael Eisner, Paul Allen and Mark Cuban. LeBron has talked about wanting to one day be a billionaire.

## Chapter 14. Free Throws

There's something LeBron James would not want anyone to know. Unless you are a basketball player, it may not seem that important. But if you are, you'd never want to admit it. In fact, you never *will* admit it, because the situation will just grow worse. Here's the deal: During parts of his career, LeBron did not want to go to the free throw line.

Why?

Because he didn't have confidence in his shot from the foul line. That's hard to believe, because the free throw should be just that—free points. It's a free shot from 15 feet with no one guarding you. It's the freedom to wait up to 10 seconds to shoot. It's freedom to line the ball up any way you'd like in your hands.

It means you are free to take a deep breath ...

Or not.

You can bounce the ball once ... twice ... three times ...

Or not.

You can think about anything you want ...

Or think nothing at all.

You can shoot a jumper as NBA great Hal Greer did at the foul line ...

You can take a set shot with your feet flat on the floor ...

You can even attempt an underhanded shot, as Rick Barry did ...

It's all up to you.

The game stops. The official hands you the ball. Everyone lines up and watches.

Opposing players aren't supposed to yell or distract you in any way once you're at the foul line with the ball.

**At times, putting LeBron on the free throw line was the best way to defend against him.**

Here's the hard part: If you miss a free throw, there is no one to blame but yourself. You probably have watched games where good players seem to lose concentration at the foul line, their shots clanging off the rim.

You wonder, "How can they miss shots like that? But they do.

When you're LeBron James and you're the star of the team, the *last* thing that you should do is miss free throws. You can drive and dunk over two guys. You can snake your way up the court, dribbling right, then left. You can dribble through your legs and around your back. You can freeze some defenders in their sneakers, making it appear they are cemented to the floor. You can fake so well defenders sometimes fall down attempting to stay with you. You can make shots that even you can't explain how you did it. You just made it up as you went along. It just happened, pure instinct. You are an athlete, and an athlete makes plays that defy description. Sometimes it happens so fast that not even the slow-motion, instant replay cameras can do it justice.

But not at the foul line, where the camera and the human eye reveal it all.

Some nine-year-old kids can make 45 of 50 free throws. So can some 60-year-olds. We are talking boys and girls, men and women. We're talking

**MVP SEASON MOMENTS**

A better supporting cast made it easier for LeBron to get to the basket during his MVP season.

PLAIN DEALER PHOTOGRAPH | JOHN KUNTZ

all sizes and ages. They may not be able to dribble the ball six times and make a lay-up on the run, but they can regularly swish free throws.

So what's the problem?

You'll never hear LeBron talk about any of this. He's a man who denies that pressure even exists.

"I hear the word 'pressure' all the time," LeBron once said. "There is a lot of pressure on me, but I don't put a lot of pressure on myself. I feel if I play my game, it will take care of itself."

That sounds good but it's a total rationalization that has no basis in reality.

Every player has, at some point, lost the battle with pressure. Yes, athletes hate it when fans and media people say they "choked," meaning their throats grew tight, their hands sweated and they failed to perform as they normally do. But choking is real. Hall of Fame NBA Coach Pat Riley has said that everyone chokes at some point. It could be the salesman who fails to close the deal when he can't find the right words. It can be the parent who sits down for an important meeting with her child, but becomes frustrated and loses her temper, rather than thoughtfully delivering the message she intended the child to hear. It can be anyone on a project, staring at a blank piece of paper, unable to put down a word as a deadline comes.

And yes, it can even be a great basketball player missing a free throw.

"Choking sometimes occurs because players do not know themselves," wrote Riley in his excellent book, "The Winner Within." "While putting on a good front, inside they really have little self-confidence. This can stop a player from ever proving himself to the fullest or going all out to develop his skills … He puts a performance cap on himself. Another result of a player not knowing himself is that he will think he is ready for a challenge when he hasn't properly prepared for it. The challenge is beyond his level of preparation."

Former Cavs coach Paul Silas noticed that at a certain point in LeBron's rookie season, he "began to shy away from contact." LeBron would drive to the basket, defenders would challenge him—and LeBron would fall away on his shot, rather than go up strong

**The scouting report on LeBron says to foul him hard, which sometimes means pain.**

and take a chance of being hit by the defender.

It was not because he was physically fearful of injury.

"He was just at a point where he was not making his free throws," recalled Silas.

LeBron didn't want to go to the foul line a lot because he was missing more than he thought he should. And, as Riley wrote, he put a "performance cap" on himself by not drawing fouls—something he does nearly as well as anyone in the league. Drawing fouls is good because it not only leads to free shots for LeBron and extra points for his team, but it saddles the opponents with personal fouls—perhaps leading the opposing coach to take some

of his players out of the game. It can put the opposition in the "penalty," leading to even more free throws for LeBron's team.

In LeBron's first two seasons, he ranked 15th and then 10th in total free throws attempted. Hard to believe, but in the next four years, he ranked exactly *third* each season in free throw attempts.

Part of the reason the number of trips to the foul line increased is that officials became used to Le-Bron's style. Yes, it means giving him some "star calls" on plays that could go either way—a personal foul on the defender, or a charging foul on LeBron. Officials deny that stars receive a break on those plays, but most coaches and players have a different opinion.

Here's a look at LeBron James at the foul line with the Cavs:

| SEASON | GAMES | ATTEMPTS | MADE | % |
|---|---|---|---|---|
| 2003–04 | 79 | 460 | 347 | .754 |
| 2004–05 | 80 | 636 | 477 | .750 |
| 2005–06 | 79 | 814 | 601 | .738 |
| 2006–07 | 78 | 701 | 489 | .698 |
| 2007–08 | 75 | 771 | 549 | .712 |
| 2008–09 | 81 | 762 | 594 | .780 |

LeBron's free throw attempts rose dramatically in his first three seasons, from 460 to 636 to 814. Part of the reason was a rule change made before the 2004–05 season. In the late 1990s and early in the 2000s, teams were having trouble scoring 100 points per game. Many final scores were in the 80s, sometimes even the 70s. Coaches were demanding their players defend by pushing, holding, shoving and any other ploy they could get away with. The belief was officials would not call most fouls because to do so would lead to a parade to the free throw line and result in a very choppy, unappealing game to watch. But to the league's credit, a mandate came down to outlaw hand-checking. In the past, a defender put his hand on a player's back, and would "steer" him away from the hoop as he tried to drive. Now, you no longer could put your hands on a player when he was away from the basket. The new rule meant there was no way to stop a guy from driving to the basket unless you could get in front of him. This meant LeBron now could get inside—and draw fouls—much more easily.

That's a problem, though, if you're having trouble finding a comfort zone at the foul line.

Riley talks about how choking results from "the challenge being beyond his level of preparation."

LeBron is a routine-oriented person, like many NBA players. His game day approach is scripted and he follows it closely. When it gets altered, he is upset. But when it came to free throw shooting, he was all over the place. He often changed his free throw and shooting routines vastly during the early seasons. This is particularly obvious in comparison with a player like LeBron's teammate Mo Williams. The Cavs guard, who is one of the better free throw shooters in the NBA, has not altered his free throw

routine since he was a sophomore in high school. His form is nearly perfect, and it is the same all the time.

Not so for LeBron.

Many fans would notice it at the foul line. During one season, he actually angled himself slightly so that he was not square—in a straight line—as he faced the basket for a free throw. That often leads the shot to drift slightly, rather than head directly over the front of the rim. In another season, he started doing deep knee bends before taking the free throw. Another year, he would kiss his two wrists before shooting. He was kissing the tattoos on his wrists that listed his mother's name and his longtime girlfriend Savannah's name. It was a calming influence, he said. But it had him switching the ball in and out of each hand and not looking at the rim. He may have copied this from one of his friends and mentors, Jason Kidd. Kidd famously used to blow a kiss at the foul line, supposedly to his wife in the stands (he stopped it after he got divorced a couple years ago). But when Kidd did it he never took his eyes off the rim. Kidd is a 78 percent career free throw shooter, above the NBA average of 76 percent.

Former Cavalier Mark Price, set the NBA record with a career average of 90 percent at the foul line.

At one point early in the 2006–07 season, LeBron had made only 59 of 98 free throws, for 60 percent. This was during his wrist-kissing period.

"Right now, I'm in Strugglesville," he said at the time. "I'm just trying to make them. I've shot in the high 70s my whole career and in the 80s in high school. It has never been a problem for me, and it's not going to be a problem now. I just have to go up there and make them."

Let's take a look at LeBron as a free throw shooter in high school.

| SEASON | ATTEMPTS | MADE | % |
|---|---|---|---|
| 1999–00 | 74 | 59 | .797 |
| 2000–01 | 173 | 123 | .711 |
| 2001–02 | 182 | 108 | .593 |
| 2002–03 | 118 | 80 | .678 |
| Career | 547 | 370 | .676 |

As a freshman, he was at his best at .797. He dropped to .711 as a sophomore. Anything over 70 percent is good for a high school player early in his career. But LeBron really fell apart as a free throw shooter his junior year, dropping to .593. It also was a season when he took the most free throws of his career. As a senior, he was up to .678.

In his pro career, his percentage dropped over his first four seasons, from .754 to .750 to .738 to .698.

At one point in 2007, as he was under 70 percent for the season, LeBron admitted: "It can be mental sometimes, and right now it is. At practice, I don't miss. I get in the game, and I miss."

The NBA free throw average most seasons is in the .765 range. It wasn't until his MVP season of 2008–09, when he connected at a career-best .780 pace, that he was above the NBA average.

With the exception of big men such as Wilt Chamberlain (.511), Shaquille O'Neal (.525) and even Tim Duncan (.685), great players often make more than 80 percent of their free throws. Here's a sample:

| NAME | CAREER % | NAME | CAREER % |
|---|---|---|---|
| Mark Price | .904 | Chris Bosh | .795 |
| Steve Nash | .899 | Walt Frazier | .786 |
| Rick Barry | .893 | Dave Cowens | .783 |
| Ray Allen | .890 | Kevin Garnett | .782 |
| Reggie Miller | .888 | Allen Iverson | .780 |
| Larry Bird | .886 | Julius Erving | .777 |
| Magic Johnson | .848 | Lenny Wilkens | .774 |
| Chris Paul | .848 | Dwyane Wade | .772 |
| Kobe Bryant | .840 | Moses Malone | .769 |
| Michael Jordan | .835 | Isiah Thomas | .759 |
| George Gervin | .821 | LeBron James | .738 |
| Paul Pierce | .798 | Charles Barkley | .735 |
| Carmelo Anthony | .796 | Tony Parker | .728 |
| | | Scottie Pippen | .704 |

So why does LeBron have such wide swings in his free throw shooting, and why doesn't he shoot as well at the line as most elite players?

The answer may partly be that he's ambidextrous. Although he plays right-handed, he's actually left-handed. He writes left-handed. He shoots bank shots driving to the basket as well with his left hand as he does with his right. But his jump shot is always right-handed. Being able to shoot inside with either hand is a huge advantage because the defender does not know which hand he will use—making his shot harder to block. But when the game stops, and when LeBron goes to the foul line to take a shot that is pure rote and routine, zero creativity or spontaneity is needed, then

maybe this ability to shoot with either hand is a liability. Sometimes, LeBron starts at the line with the ball in his left hand. He might spin it and sometimes even dribble it with his left hand. As he lines up, he might set it against his left hip—and then bring it over to his right hand. Most experts will tell you that you need to set it on the right hand. Keep everything on the right side, the side where you plan to shoot the ball.

In LeBron's MVP season of 2008–09, he raised that total to a career-high .780. He stopped kissing his wrists, staring at the ceiling, taking extra bounces. Shooting coach Chris Jent helped LeBron "clean up" his shot, as scouts call it. That means he cut out the extra movement, and the result was a more consistent shot, more free points. It was the first time in his six-year pro career that he was a better than average NBA free-throw shooter. He also made a huge jump from .712 to .780.

He also dealt better with pressure.

As Pat Riley also wrote in "The Winner Within": "Somewhere along the way we have to stop being afraid of the consequences. Because when you go for something significant … consequences become irrelevant. Nothing matters except that we are in this together."

You can see LeBron's growth in the playoffs at the free throw line:

| YEAR | ATTEMPTS PER GAME | % |
|---|---|---|
| 2006 | 9.1 | .737 |
| 2007 | 9.8 | .757 |
| 2008 | 12.8 | .731 |
| 2009 | 14.2 | .749 |

LeBron was willing to drive in the lane more each year, take more fouls and attempt more shots. While his percentage didn't change much over the four years of playoff basketball (ranging between .731 and .759), his confidence in making plays that lead to free throws—helping his team in the process—made a dramatic rise. LeBron ceased "being afraid of the consequences." NBA fans saw it in big ways as he became a leader, not only of the Cavaliers, but also of the U.S. Olympic team—at the age of 24. But it's there in little ways, too, as in the way LeBron worked on his free throws. And that's a part of his evolution into an MVP that is rarely mentioned.

## MVP SEASON MOMENTS

Where LeBron took his shots from the field, some career milestones and single game highlights.

PLAIN DEALER GRAPHIC | DENNIS MANOLOFF

### The King on the Court

LeBron James scored **2,304** points in his MVP 2008-2009 regular season, for an average of **28.4.** He averaged 27.5 through six seasons, extending his franchise record for points (12,993).

He went **789-of-1,613** from the field. The **.489** percentage was best of his career (previous: .484 in 2007-2008). It improved his career percentage to .471.

He was **132-of-384** from 3-point range, a career high (previous: 127 in 2005-2006). The **.344** percentage is second-best of his career (best: .351 in 2004-2005).

LBJ's 789 field goals broke down this way:

| | |
|---|---|
| 33 feet: | 1 |
| 32 feet: | 0 |
| 31 feet: | 0 |
| 30 feet: | 1 |
| 29 feet: | 1 |
| 28 feet: | 7 |
| 27 feet: | 11 |
| 26 feet: | 33 |
| 25 feet: | 53 |
| 24 feet: | 17 |
| 23 feet: | 20 |
| 22 feet: | 30 |
| 21 feet: | 29 |
| 20 feet: | 30 |
| 19 feet: | 25 |
| 18 feet: | 15 |
| 17 feet: | 15 |
| 16 feet: | 14 |
| 15 feet: | 8 |
| 14 feet: | 9 |
| 13 feet: | 2 |
| 12 feet: | 5 |
| 11 feet: | 2 |
| 10 feet: | 4 |
| 9 feet: | 3 |
| 8 feet: | 17 |
| 7 feet: | 10 |
| 6 feet: | 12 |
| 5 feet: | 8 |
| 4 feet: | 6 |
| 3 feet: | 4 |
| 2 feet: | 1 |
| 1 foot: | 12 |
| Layups: | 259 |
| Dunks: | 125 |

Of his **125** dunks,
45 were in the first quarter,
19 in the second,
38 in the third and
23 in the fourth.

He had 38 dunks
in the first 20 games,
32 in the next 20,
32 in the next 20 and
23 in the final 21.

**Jan.15,2008:** LeBron scored 51 points and made seven three-pointers in a win in Memphis.

**March5,2008:** LeBron scored 50 points at Madison Square Garden to beat the New York Knicks, hitting a three-pointer in the final minute to reach the number.

**Feb.4,2009:** LeBron scored 52 points with nine rebounds and 11 assists in a win over the Knicks. It was believed to be the first 50-point triple double since Wilt Chamberlain in 1968, but a day after the game the NBA took away one rebound.

**Feb.20,2009:** LeBron scored 55 points in a win in Milwaukee and set a personal best by hitting eight three-pointers.

**March13,2009:** LeBron scored 51 points in a victory over the Kings in Sacramento in overtime.

**May9,2009:** LeBron scored 47 points with 12 rebounds and eight assists as the Cavs beat the Atlanta Hawks in Game 3 of the Eastern Conference Semifinals. The Cavs went on to sweep the series, 4-0.

**May23,2009:** LeBron made a three-pointer at the buzzer to beat the Orlando Magic in Game 2 of the Eastern Conference Finals.

# Chapter 15. **Shooting**

Many NBA fans believe that players play a lot in the summers, especially pickup games against other pros. At times they do. A young Michael Jordan had a "love of the game" clause written into one of his early contracts with the Bulls, allowing him to play in any game, anywhere in the off-season, and his contract would not be voided if he were injured in those pickup games. But by his late 20s, Jordan discovered that pickup games don't make you a better player. Being in the weight room does. Being in the gym alone, shooting, does. Setting up chairs in a gym and dribbling around them with his left hand (weaker than the right) paid more dividends than dunking on some old buddies from Duke and North Carolina. Working with a coach to help his shooting was the ticket to a better performance. Putting together a systematic off-season program enabled Jordan to go from an erratic outside shooter to a solid one, and it set the stage for him to drive as well to his left as he did his right.

It was solitary practice that made Jordan a five-time MVP. The same type of regimen would lead LeBron to his first MVP award in 2009.

Here's the remarkable part of this story that is often ignored: LeBron was 22 years old when the Cavs lost in the 2007 NBA Finals. How many 22-year-olds are willing to look in the mirror and not make excuses for their failures? How many professional athletes are ready to admit that despite their huge contracts, despite already having made more money than they could ever spend, despite all the fame they already had, they might have to work even harder than they ever had before?

No coach, no parent, no friend can convince a player to do that.

It must come from inside. It must come from a

**In an effort to improve, LeBron started devoting his summers to working with coaches.**

sense of pride combining with a desire to be great simply because that is his calling — not to please anyone else, or to secure a new contract or more commercials. It's sensing that there is a calling on his life, a sense of destiny that he must pursue. So two weeks after losing in the 2007 NBA Finals, LeBron sat down with a man named Chris Jent.

Jent had been hired by Cavaliers coach Mike Brown at the start of the 2006 regular season. He had been looking for work after being fired as interim head coach by the Orlando Magic when that team made coaching changes after a disappointing 2004–05 season. Jent bonded with LeBron quickly. LeBron liked how Jent could be serious at times and also have fun at times, challenging him in games of HORSE but also working him out hard. Their personalities matched. Plus, LeBron remembered Jent from his playing days at Ohio State, and LeBron, a true hoops fan,

PLAIN DEALER PHOTOGRAPH | ROADELL HICKMAN

**Cavaliers assistant coach Chris Jent helped LeBron refine his free-throw routine.**

recalled that Jent had a nice game, especially as a shooter. There was instant respect. He liked how Jent instructed him but did not force his ideas on him. That was true of free throw shooting, where LeBron had sometimes struggled. Jent offered tips, but also let LeBron decide when to implement them. Jent quickly recognized that LeBron has to come around to ideas. He is only going to do something when he's ready. You have to show him the value and let him understand. LeBron values that understanding. "I like Chris and I trust Chris," he has often said.

The two are a fascinating match. Jent was never a phenom. He did play for the Ohio State Buckeyes in the 1990s, but he was not a star, not drafted out of college. He played only six regular-season NBA games, for a total of 88 minutes, then chased the game to Italy, Spain and Australia. A 6-foot-7, 220-pound basketball junkie, as an assistant coach Jent still loved to play pickup games with Cavaliers players and others after practice. LeBron noticed that Jent was not especially athletic, but

PLAIN DEALER PHOTOGRAPH | JOHN KUNTZ

the man could shoot. He had a sweet lefty jumper — high arch, nice rotation, perfect release off the fingertips. Jent was there before practice and after practice, willing to work with any player — especially on shooting. But he wasn't pushy, didn't act as if he knew everything about shooting. He had a nice, quiet way of making suggestions, offering encouragement.

When LeBron realized he needed a shooting coach, he could have turned to one of several men who have made an industry of working with players. They are consultants, not affiliated with any team — private tutors. But LeBron knew that some of them might use a relationship with a young star to help attract other clients and build their business. He has always been wary of people using his name or his fame for their personal gain. Jent was different. Jent had a wife, three kids and a pure love of the game. The gym was his sanctuary, the dribble of the ball, his heartbeat. He was like some of the teachers that LeBron had had in high school; they were truly in it for the kids — for the satisfaction that comes from helping another person learn. Jent was a purist, and he was not the sort of man to brag about any relationship with LeBron.

Jent often played 3-on-3 with some of the Cavaliers' reserve players after practices or before games when they wanted extra work. LeBron watched Jent swish shots over younger players. Teammate Daniel Gibson told LeBron that Jent knew a lot about shooting, so LeBron asked Jent if he would be willing to work with him in the summer of 2007.

Two weeks after the end of the 2007 playoffs, LeBron arranged for Jent to fly to Connecticut, where LeBron was on vacation. The two men sat down and formulated a summer regimen intended to make LeBron a better shooter. They began working in a gym out there. LeBron then went to Los Angeles to tape some commercials, and he had Jent travel with him so they could continue the workouts. During breaks, LeBron and Jent would work on shooting fundamentals. At one end of the court near a basket were the photographer and staff, at the other end was an open basket with Jent and a ball — waiting for LeBron.

The shooting work with Jent was in addition to LeBron's regular conditioning.

"Six days a week, LeBron does some sort of workout; that's not counting his shooting drills," said Jent. "They do things to help his flexibility and balance. LeBron also has his own chef. He is extremely serious about being a better player."

LeBron begins his workouts by meeting with assistant trainer Mike Mancias. Sometimes, they lift weights. Sometimes, it's yoga. It always involves some stretching.

With Jent, he begins with 90 minutes of shooting drills. Most of the shots will come from 14 to 19 feet away. They begin with six different spots on the court, but also at different ranges.

Then they come back at night for more shooting.

"In the summer, he'll shoot at least once a day, probably six days a week," said Jent. "Sometimes, it will be twice a day."

Jent knows that LeBron doesn't trust most people, especially with something as important as tinkering with his jumper.

"To a player, a shot is his signature," said Jent. "It's not easy for them to change it."

But LeBron did agree to several suggestions from Jent, and that did help his free throw shooting and his jumper.

Not only do LeBron and Jent practice in Cleveland, LeBron has taken Jent on the road to continue their sessions. They'll practice in Los Angeles after he tapes commercials. They'll practice in Portland, when LeBron travels there for Nike business. They have found gyms in Washington, D.C. and New York when LeBron had appearances in those cities.

"The last two summers, LeBron was involved with the Olympic team," said Jent. "He practiced with them during the day, and we'd shoot at night."

LeBron shot .698 from the foul line in his last season before connecting with Jent. It rose to .780 in his MVP season. LeBron's field goal percentage went up from .476 to .489, his three-pointers, from .319 to .344. All in two years.

LeBron continues to work on his shooting with Jent on game days, too.

A few hours before the game, he will take 30 shots from six different spots on the on the court — and four spots in between. Then he takes another 40 shots or more near the basket, practicing short hook shots. He mixes in free throws. Chris Jent puts him through the paces.

LeBron also practices his dunks. Not dunks for a contest, but posting up on both sides of the basket, catching the ball with his back to the hoop. He then fakes one direction, spins the other — takes a quick dribble or two and then dunks. The drill also gets his legs ready for the game without making them too tired.

LeBron also takes about 100 total shots from various spots on the court during the morning shoot-around. At the end, he practices some shots from at least 35 feet. He has made several incredible long jumpers at the end of quarters. How does he do it? He does practice those shots, too. Not a lot, but he does think about how to best get off a good shot from long distance right before the buzzer. (Part of the reason LeBron's three-point shooting percentage is a not very impressive 34 percent is that he will take long shots at the end of quarters and halves. Some players won't throw up a 40-footer because they want to preserve their field goal percentage.)

In short, LeBron James' shooting improved over several years because of a four-letter word: work.

"LeBron has always been a hard-working player," said General Manager Danny Ferry. "Chris is a basketball junkie. He truly loves the game. He has helped LeBron see the little things. At the same time, Chris understands how lucky he is to work with a player that has incredible talent, wants to be the best and does the hard work needed."

"LeBron is driven to win a championship," said Jent. "Most people have no idea how hard he works. The drills we do are not natural to him. A great player practices the things that don't come easy."

> **THE LEBRON FILE**
> LeBron is one of just two players in NBA history to average at least 27 points, 6 rebounds and 6 assists for five consecutive seasons. The other was Oscar Robertson.

## MVP SEASON MOMENTS

LeBron and his teammates show cohesiveness through pregame handshakes, salutes and dances.

# Chapter 16. **Staying Strong**

During the 2008–09 season, hotel guests in various NBA cities have likely been a little jolted to see LeBron James by the pool in the mornings. Not so much because he's a celebrity, but because he just might be standing on his head. When LeBron first came into the NBA at the age of 18 he didn't even tape his ankles, sometimes ate McDonald's an hour before tip-off and his main use for ice was cooling beverages. In high school, he'd sometimes stuff himself with sugary cereals such as Fruity Pebbles, Frosted Flakes and Cinnamon Toast Crunch.

Now, LeBron often eats sushi, grilled fish, the best cuts of steak with little fat and plenty of vegetables. He watches the sugar intake, and raises the protein. Michael Jordan did much of the same thing in the middle of his career, sometimes hiring a chef on the road to come to his hotel and make meals such as bison steak with his favorite vegetables. Like Jordan, LeBron realizes a key to greatness is staying healthy, staying strong and that even the best bodies can turn bad from a lack of care.

"It's commitment," LeBron often says.

That can apply to everything from his training techniques to his diet to icing everything from his shoulders to his knees to his feet after games.

Most of all, it involves stretching — something most athletes hate.

But after five years in the NBA, LeBron embraced a wide range of measures from diet and recovery techniques. Yoga poses are an essential part of LeBron's routine every week.

"Yoga isn't just about the body, it's also about the mind and it's a technique that has really helped me," LeBron said. "You do have to focus because there's some positions that can really hurt you at

**LeBron uses a variety of methods for strengthening and protecting his body.**

times if you aren't focused and breathing right."

From the "thunderbolt pose" to the "hero pose" to even "downward facing dog," LeBron has become a devout believer in the benefits of yoga. He and Cavs assistant athletic trainer Mike Mancias have been developing a regimen over the last two years. LeBron became serious about yoga in the summer of 2007 when Mancias was with him for much of the Team USA events in Las Vegas and China. During the season, they'd carve out time at least once a week, and sometimes more, for the practice. Often it happens at team hotels on the road and the two prefer to do it outside if possible. The two also do some Pilates exercises.

"He tries to focus on things that will help him and that his body needs, especially for balance and

**Cavs athletic trainer Mike Mancias puts LeBron through a stretching routine before each game.**

to strengthen his core," said Mancias. "Yoga is an activity that encompasses all that. It's total body and it helps him mentally, too. Flexibility is important to him and we've tried to incorporate all of that into a routine."

Basketball players have been experimenting with yoga for decades. Kareem Abdul-Jabbar was perhaps the first high-profile player to embrace it. In recent years, Shaquille O'Neal has used it at times to increase flexibility in his legs. Phil Jackson, who is famous for his alternative techniques, used it as a player to help with back problems and had the Bulls go through a series of yoga classes throughout the 1997–98 championship season. The theory is that basketball players tend to be strong in certain areas, such as the legs and arms, due to the nature of the game. But all the repetitive motion can build up tension and limit flexibility in some joints and large muscles.

LeBron started getting into the importance of stretching during his third season. Partially inspired by then-teammate Alan Henderson — who extended his 12-year career by using elastic bands and a large inflatable ball in a stretching routine — LeBron began to devote himself to making sure he was limber. At the time, he was also bothered by some lower back spasms, which nearly forced him out of a playoff game against the Wizards in 2006. That and a couple of nasty ankle sprains got LeBron focused on doing things to maximize his physical tools. Stretching with bands after practices and games slowly developed into using yoga. The positions increase flexibility in areas athletes don't always pay attention to, but that basketball players especially need to — areas such as ankles, shoulders and hips. Fans can surely remember times when LeBron appeared to have suffered serious ankle injuries only to shake them off. Some of that may be due to the freakish size of LeBron's joints, but some of it may be from those targeted workouts.

During the 2008–09 season, he flipped over backwards while chasing a loose ball in Phoenix. It looked like he may have hurt his neck doing it, but in reality it was sort of like the salamba sarvanga-

## A TYPICAL LEBRON GAME DAY

**MORNING**
Stretching
Strategy sessions, drills and shooting with
teammates and coaches
Film work

**AFTERNOON**
Lunch and hydration
Nap

**PREGAME**
Small meal
A mixture of weight training, massage therapy,
stretching, ankle taping and shooting

**POSTGAME**
Ice bath for feet, ice packs on lower back and
sometimes shoulders.
Small meal, often chicken, sushi and/or fruit
with recovery drinks.

sana, or shoulder stand, he'd worked on a day before.

"It is something that really can help your balance," LeBron said. "I had some lower back problems a few years ago and once I started to do the yoga, it has helped them go away for now. Of course we can stretch, but stretching only goes so far."

It's part of a package LeBron now employs. He gets massages on most game days, gets his ankles heavily taped, wears a padded vest under his jersey to protect his ribs, and ices his feet and lower back after every game and contact workout. It includes an overall better series of eating habits and weight training, which LeBron is now more devoted to than ever.

"People don't see everything that he does. He's focused on doing everything for his body that will help him succeed," Mancias said. "The proof is what he's been showing on the court."

As LeBron has experienced the benefits, he's become an advocate of yoga, Pilates and massage therapy that he does with the Cavs and their support staff.

"I've been blessed with a lot of physical talent and a strong body," LeBron said. "I have focused on working hard to maximize those gifts."

PLAIN DEALER PHOTOGRAPH | ROADELL HICKMAN

## Chapter 17. **Chasing Michael Jordan**

When Michael Jordan was 21 years old, he was a rookie with the Chicago Bulls. When LeBron James was 21 years old, he was in his third pro season with the Cleveland Cavaliers.

Basketball fans in Northeast Ohio might be excused for thinking LeBron James has been around forever; they have been hearing about him ever since 2000, when he was a freshman sensation at Akron's St. Vincent-St. Mary High School. But it's worth remembering that at the same age that Jordan was starting his college career for Dean Smith at the University of North Carolina, LeBron was already a rookie with the Cavaliers. It doesn't matter that LeBron looked older than 18 when he came into the NBA, or sounded so much older when he was 22 and the Cavaliers were in the NBA Finals for the first time in the franchise's history. Or that he was already playing like a 10-year NBA veteran on the other side of 30 — before his 25th birthday.

In basketball terms, that makes him very, very young.

That's why some early comparisons between Jordan and LeBron were unfair. Members of the media had one eye on a Michael Jordan in his middle 30s who had six championship rings. They had another eye on a LeBron James in his early-to-middle 20s, wondering why he wasn't measuring up to Jordan. They forget it took Jordan seven years to win that first title. Or that it wasn't until Jordan's fourth season that his Chicago Bulls finally won a playoff series! There is a famous picture of Jordan hugging a championship trophy, tears pouring out of his eyes. The year was 1991, it was Jordan's first NBA title. It came seven years into his career. He was 28 years old. He had been the Rookie of the Year in 1985, the Defensive Player of the year in 1988, and the MVP in 1988.

He also had five scoring titles next to his name. But heading into the 1991 playoffs, he had not won a championship. Not one. Even after he was named MVP for 1991, he still was in the midst of the postseason, chasing that first championship. He also was on his fourth coach (Phil

> **THE LEBRON FILE**
> LeBron had a triple double in his first-ever playoff game, against Washington on April 22, 2006. He had 32 points, 11 rebounds and 11 assists.

**LeBron's performance in the 2007 playoffs against the Detroit Pistons had many comparing him to a young Michael Jordan.**

PLAIN DEALER PHOTOGRAPH | JOHN KUNTZ

Jackson) in seven years. In fact, his team had never even reached the NBA Finals in his first six seasons. There were more than a few moments when Jordan wondered if it ever would happen, if he'd ever win a title. Some critics insisted he was too great of a scorer to be a champion. He dominated the ball, took too many shots, caused his teammates to stand and watch rather than move and be ready to shoot.

Now, most of that is forgotten.

Jordan is simply considered one of the greatest winners of all time, in the same select circle as Bill Russell, Larry Bird and Magic Johnson. But no one knew that was coming in his first six years, or even after he won that first title at the age of 28.

Which is why it is unwise to make any sweeping statements about the future of LeBron James when it comes to championship.

Let's review a bit:

1. Jordan was the No. 3 pick in the 1984 NBA draft. He joined a Bulls team that was 27-55 and had been to the playoffs only once in the previous seven years. LeBron was the top pick in the 2003 draft, coming to a Cavs team that was worse than those pre-Jordan Bulls: 17-65. Those Cavs had been to the playoffs only once in the previous seven years.

2. In Jordan's rookie season, the Bulls improved from 27 to 38 victories, losing in the first round of the playoffs. As a rookie, LeBron took the Cavs from 17 to 35 victories, missing the playoffs.

3. In his second season, LeBron took the Cavs from 34 to 42 wins, missing the playoffs. Jordan sat out 65 games (64 of them with a broken foot). The Bulls dropped from 38 to 30 victories, made the playoffs anyway, and were swept in the first round.

4. In his third season, LeBron raised the Cavs from 42 to 50 wins. In his first playoff appearance, the Cavs went to the second round, losing to Detroit in seven games. Jordan's third year saw a 40-42 record and a loss in the first round. At this point, Jordan had appeared in

10 postseason games, losing nine. Jordan won his first MVP award.

5. In his fourth season, LeBron led the Cavs to a 50-32 record. They advanced to the NBA Finals for the first time in franchise history, being swept by San Antonio. In Jordan's fourth season, the Bulls finally won 50 games. They also finally won a playoff series, beating the Cavs in 1988. The Bulls lost to the Detroit Pistons in the second round.

6. In his fifth season, LeBron led the Cavs to a 45-37 record; they lost to Boston in the second round. In Jordan's fifth season, the Bulls were 47-35. They beat the Cavs in the first round on the last-second play known as "The Shot", and advanced to the Eastern Conference Finals, losing to Detroit.

7. In his sixth season, LeBron led the Cavs to a 66-16 record and they lost in the Eastern Conference Finals to Orlando. LeBron won his first MVP award. In his sixth season, Jordan's Bulls were 55-27. They lost to Detroit in the Eastern Conference Finals.

Let's look at a few more things:

1. By Jordan's seventh season, not a single player remained on the Bulls' roster from his rookie year. Center Dave Corzine was the only member of Jordan's first Bulls team to last even five seasons, then he was traded away. The only Cavs player still with the Cavs for the duration of the LeBron Era as he began his seventh season in 2009–10 was center Zydrunas Ilgauskas. The point is both teams had to go through a lot of players to find the right combination to blend with their stars.

2. Every player publicly says he loves to win, but that is not the real priority of some players running around in NBA uniforms. When Jordan joined the Bulls, some players on the team had drug problems. There also were players such as Quintin Dailey and Orlando Woolridge who wanted their shots and points, and were not exactly thrilled to share the spotlight with Jordan. In the early years of the Cavs,

**Jordan blocked the Cavs' path to a title in the '80s and '90s, as a young LeBron watched on TV.**

players had attitude and discipline problems. Ricky Davis resented the attention given to LeBron. Even later in the LeBron Era, when the Cavs advanced to the 2007 NBA Finals, Larry Hughes was unhappy despite earning $12 million. He was traded in February 2008, came

back to town as a member of the Jordan-less, losing Bulls and talked about how basketball in Cleveland was "no fun," and how they "were just into winning." He mentioned how he just wanted to "play my game" and have fun.

3. In Jordan's first three years, the Bulls had three coaches in Kevin Loughery, Stan Albeck and Doug Collins. They also had a 1-9 record in the playoffs. LeBron also had three coaches in three seasons — Paul Silas, Brendan Malone and Mike Brown. They missed the playoffs the first two years, then lost in the second round in Year 3 of the LeBron Era. As frustrating as those seasons were to LeBron and Cavs fans, the agony and turmoil in Chicago over Jordan's first three seasons seemed even worse. The Bulls didn't even have a winning regular-season record in any of those years.

4. It wasn't until Jordan's fourth season that the parts of the championship run were coming into place, as Horace Grant and Scottie Pippen joined the team. Neither averaged more than eight points per game. The other key players on that 1987–88 Bulls team were Charles Oakley, John Paxson, Sam Vincent, Brad Sellers and Dave Corzine.

5. It took the Big Three of Jordan, Pippen and Grant four years, until 1991, to win their first NBA title. That was Jordan's seventh season. He was 28 years old. From Year 4 to Year 7 for the Bulls, the only player who remained with the Big Three to win a title was John Paxson. A key trade was Charles Oakley for Bill Cartwright, giving the Bulls a low-post defender they lacked. As the seventh season opened, the Cavs made their own Cartwright deal, importing massive center Shaquille O'Neal to man the middle.

6. It was Phil Jackson who coached the Bulls to that first title, and he would win five more in Chicago. He was Jordan's fourth coach in seven years. Jordan also had two general managers: Rod Thorn, who drafted him, and Jerry Krause, who later replaced Thorn. It was Krause who hired Jackson. LeBron also had two general managers: Jim Paxson, who had

the job when the Cavs won the 2003 draft lottery, and Danny Ferry, who was hired in 2005. That same summer of 2005, Mike Brown became LeBron's third coach.

Since we're taking a stroll through history, here are some reasons some other players are not in this discussion. It comes down to two words: supporting cast. These guys joined teams who had at least one All-Star:

1. As the first decade of the 21st century came to a close, the main debate about who is the NBA's best player came to two choices: Kobe Bryant of the Los Angeles Lakers and LeBron. Bryant did not win a title in his first three pro seasons. Then he was on three consecutive championship teams from 2000–02. That happened when Phil Jackson was hired as coach and he found a way to mesh Bryant with Shaquille O'Neal, the center who was picked as one the game's Top 50 players ever while still active. It was only in 2009 that Bryant could claim a title without O'Neal. That was Bryant's 13th year in the NBA.

2. Boston's Larry Bird won three titles, and did it with two Hall of Famers as teammates — Robert Parish and Kevin McHale. His last two title teams also had Dennis Johnson, who should be in the Hall of Fame, in the backcourt.

3. Magic Johnson won five titles, all with the Lakers and all with center Kareem Abdul-Jabbar, perhaps one of the 10 greatest ever to play in the NBA. To say "Hall of Famer" is only to begin to praise the man who has scored more points than anyone in NBA history. Johnson also won three of those titles with Hall of Famer James Worthy as a teammate.

4. Bill Russell has 11 championship rings. He never played on a Boston team without other Hall of Famers. One of his championship teams had six Hall of Famers on the roster, counting Russell. To be fair, Boston never won a title until Russell arrived, but the defensive specialist at center never had to worry

about scoring. There were always plenty of sharp shooters in Celtic green to help.

5. Wilt Chamberlain won only two titles: one with Hall of Famer Jerry West and the Lakers in 1972, his only title. The other was with the 1967 Philadelphia 76ers, a team with Hall of Famers Hal Greer and Billy Cunningham.

6. Julius Erving had one NBA title with Philadelphia in 1983 with Hall of Fame center Moses Malone.

7. Oscar Robertson won his only title with Milwaukee in 1971; Abdul-Jabbar was the center.

8. Kareem Abdul-Jabbar has six titles next to his name: five with Magic Johnson, one with Oscar Robertson.

9. San Antonio's Tim Duncan has four championship rings: two with Hall of Famer David Robinson, three with All-Star guard Tony Parker. One of those title teams had Parker (a safe bet to be a future Hall of Famer) and Robinson.

10. Hakeem Olajuwon won two titles with Houston. Those were in 1994 and 1995, when Jordan was not with the Bulls and played minor league baseball. Jordan returned for the 1995 playoffs but was not in top basketball condition. Olajuwon did not have a strong supporting cast, except maybe Clyde Drexler, acquired at the trading deadline and past his prime. So his two titles are significant, even if some would put a Jordan asterisk next to it. A back-in-shape Jordan won three more titles from 1996–98.

So what does all this say about Jordan and LeBron?

No matter how great the player, he needs help to win. Often, he must have a Hall of Fame caliber player in the same lineup, even if that player is aging and not at his peak. Or he must have a rising star.

LeBron doesn't want any part of this debate. The longer he is in the NBA, the more of an appreciation he has gained of Jordan's six championship rings.

"There will never be another Michael Jordan," he said. "You'll drive yourself crazy trying be another Michael."

## MVP SEASON MOMENTS

The Cavs use four or five different uniforms during the season, and fans buy up the "James" versions.

PLAIN DEALER PHOTOGRAPH | TRACY BOULIAN

# Chapter 18. "I Have to be 10 Times Better"

LeBron James' journey to the 2009 Most Valuable Player award began in silence.

It was the day after the Cleveland Cavaliers were swept out of the 2007 NBA Finals by the San Antonio Spurs. As is usual at the end of the season, the players arrived at the arena to clean out their lockers and talk a bit to the coaches and media about the season.

LeBron had nothing to say — to anyone.

He was exhausted. He was discouraged. He didn't take much satisfaction from the Cavs knocking out the Detroit Pistons in the 2007 Eastern Conference Finals. What bothered LeBron was knowing that the Cavaliers were not good enough to win a championship. He'd never say it, but when any serious basketball person thought of a starting backcourt for a contending team — Sasha Pavlovic and Larry Hughes didn't come to mind. In fact, it was amazing the Cavs had won 50 games with those guards. That they had knocked off Detroit in six games in the Eastern Conference Finals. Or that a team with only three notable big men in Drew Gooden, Zydrunas Ilgauskas and Anderson Varejao had even played in the Finals.

The team needed work, and LeBron knew it.

He looked back at the San Antonio sweep and knew it wasn't all the fault (or lack of talent) of his teammates. In those four games, he shot 36 percent from the field. In those four games, he made 22 turnovers. In those four games, he couldn't get to the basket as he wanted; he couldn't find the touch on his jumper.

In those four games, he felt very human.

**The Spurs shut down LeBron in the NBA Finals — which inspired him to improve his game.**

"I need to definitely get better," LeBron said immediately after the Finals. "Once I get better, our team will automatically get better, and I know that. I have to do everything that I've done well and try to improve in order for us to be a better team next year."

LeBron noticed the Spurs were daring him to shoot ... not just long distance from three-point range, but closer to the basket. They gave him open 18-footers. Open 15-footers. He even struggled at the foul line, making only 69 percent.

"We went up against a better team in this series, and everybody has to be better coming into next season," LeBron said. "I have to be ten times better. Our team has to be ten times better. We have to be better. Me, as an individual, I have to be much better on and off the court, and that will carry our team to higher levels. I think it starts with me first and then it will trickle down to everybody else."

This is where it's so easy to forget that LeBron was only 22 years old, so easy to forget that athletes of any age tend to make excuses for themselves and their teams — or settle for finishing second. It would have been natural for LeBron to think about how no one expected the Cavs to beat Detroit in the Eastern Conference Finals, much less play for a title. It would have been tempting for most

## MVP SEASON MOMENTS

In the 2008–09 season, LeBron led the Cavaliers to a team record 27 road game wins.

PLAIN DEALER PHOTOGRAPH | TRACY BOULIAN

players to shrug off the poor shooting in the Finals as a product of not having much help from his teammates. Larry Hughes was hurt, having played only two games and scored a grand total of two points. Zydrunas Ilgauskas had had a rough series, shooting only 45 percent and averaging 7.8 points. Other than Drew Gooden (12.8 points, 8.3 rebounds), no other Cavalier even played his normal game against the Spurs.

More than a few players in LeBron's position would say, *Hey, I carried this team on my back all season. I had to score 29 of the last 30 points in Game 5 at Detroit to even put us in position to win the Piston series.*

But he didn't. Nor did he ever mention his stats from the final four games of the Detroit series — all victories — when he averaged an eye-popping 31.3 points, 9.8 rebounds and 8.8 assists. Those are Hall of Fame-level numbers.

LeBron played more total minutes during the 2006–07 regular season than anyone in the NBA. He was asked about being tired as a reason for his poor performance in the Finals, but at the press conference, he said: "I felt great throughout the season. Everyone is injured at this point, everyone is a little fatigued. It's not an excuse ... My turnovers are uncharacteristic, a lot of unforced errors, me losing the ball or making bad passes. It's all things I can control, and I wasn't able to do that."

As a basketball player, this was the first time that LeBron believed he had failed.

Not that he had expected the Cavs to beat the Spurs, although LeBron goes into every game, every series, convinced he can find a way to make his team win. But just as certain, LeBron never, ever, even in his worst nightmare, expected his team to be swept out in four games. This was worse than losing the state championship in his junior year at St. Vincent-St. Mary, when he failed to make a big play at the end of a close game. That was one game, one play. It hurt, and there were

**THE LEBRON FILE**
LeBron is one of three players in history to record a triple double in his first playoff game. The others were Johnny McCarthy in 1960 with the St. Louis Hawks, and Magic Johnson with the Los Angeles Lakers in 1980.

tears when it was over, but it felt more like a fluke. In that game, LeBron's team lost 71-63 to Cincinnati's Roger Bacon High School. LeBron scored 32 points, but had seven turnovers and only three rebounds and six assists.

In his heart, LeBron believed if his high school team had played a best-of-7 series with Roger Bacon, it would have won. And in his heart, LeBron knew that no matter how many games the series would be with those 2007 San Antonio Spurs, the Cavaliers would have lost.

He had struggled against that defense. To shoot 36 percent? To make 22 turnovers in those four games? To not even be sure of where he wanted to go on the court to get a shot? Over and over, those thoughts haunted him. It wasn't just that his team had been swept. He believed he had let the team down.

That trip to the 2007 NBA Finals whispered this to LeBron, "You are not good enough. Other players are better."

LeBron never said any of this out loud, but it haunted him when he took off two weeks following the season. It demanded that he realize something else — by the finals, he was physically tired, emotionally drained. He may have been one of the most unique physical specimens in the NBA, but LeBron came to the realization that not only must his game improve — but he had to get in better shape.

LeBron didn't stay on the court to watch the Spurs receive their championship trophy.

"I didn't turn around to look at it," he said. "I've seen other teams win a title before, me watching on TV. I knew what they were doing. But I didn't want to look at it."

After the series, Spurs star Tim Duncan told LeBron, "Someday, this league is going to belong to you."

Those words had significance for him, but he knew there was a long road for him to travel if he wanted to reach Duncan's MVP and championship level.

# Chapter 19. Team USA

For the first time in his life, basketball did not come easy for LeBron James. And he was playing for a coach who wasn't utterly enamored with his talent and attitude.

Welcome to the 2004 United States Olympic team.

The 19-year-old LeBron James had just won the 2004 Rookie of the Year Award. Now he was playing for the USA team coached by Larry Brown, who was trying to revive a national team that had finished an embarrassing sixth in the 2002 World Championships on its home turf in Indianapolis. Brown took over in 2003, and Team USA glided to Olympic qualification by winning a tournament in Puerto Rico. But 12 players turned down the invitation to play for the 2004 team. The Team USA committee was scrambling to secure players within a month of the start of training camp. There were five late additions, including LeBron.

LeBron was part of a group of young players who saw themselves as the future of the Olympic program and the NBA. It also included Carmelo Anthony, Dwyane Wade and Amare Stoudemire. LeBron was excited by the opportunity, and especially to play for Brown, a Hall of Fame coach. Brown had praised LeBron during his rookie season, a year when Brown had led the Detroit Pistons to a championship.

The team trained in Jacksonville, Florida. When LeBron arrived, he hooked up with veteran Allen Iverson, whom he had been introduced to while still in high school. It seemed like a good match. Iverson had been the MVP three years earlier, and he had played for Brown in Philadelphia. Brown also named Iverson as one of Team USA's captains.

**LeBron's time with Team USA made him a better player and leader, winding up with a defining performance at the 2008 Olympics in China.**

Iverson was one of the veterans LeBron admired.

But a few days after the start of camp, LeBron, Iverson and Stoudemire showed up late for a team meeting. Brown was angry. To set an example, he suspended all three for an exhibition game that week against Puerto Rico. It was out of character for LeBron, who is known for always being on time. It was a sign that he was trying to fit in and go with the crowd on the veteran team. It also was a reminder that he was only 19.

LeBron received a reasonable amount of playing time during the series of exhibition games in Europe on the way to Athens, Greece, the host city of the 2004 Olympics. But once the real Olympic games began, Brown barely played LeBron or the other young players. This was a shock to them. Brown had not spelled out their role, and they all believed they were key parts of the team. Instead, most of the minutes went to Stephon Marbury, Richard Jefferson and Lamar Odom. All played inconsistently.

THE STAR-LEDGER PHOTOGRAPH | ANDREW MILLS

**Team USA's coaches made LeBron the defensive captain — a demanding role that improved his game.**

During a stretch of games when LeBron and Wade played well, they came up with a nickname for themselves, along with Anthony and Stoudemire. They started calling themselves the "Young Guns." That didn't exactly thrill Brown, who saw it as a sign of arrogance.

LeBron played 18 minutes and had 10 points and five rebounds in a win over Australia. He thought he'd played well. But he played only six minutes in the next game against Lithuania, which Team USA lost. Then LeBron played only six minutes in the next game. Against Angola, LeBron was on the court for 27 minutes, scoring 11 points. He felt confident about his stature on the team, and the nick-

names were being tossed around again. But in the next two games of the medal round, including a loss to Argentina that ended gold medal hopes, LeBron played a total of 10 minutes.

Brown wasn't enamored with the younger players. He complained about their failures and almost seemed to be setting them up to take the blame if the Olympic team failed to grab the gold medal. He rarely said anything encouraging to them. Anthony and Stoudemire openly showed their disdain for Brown, refusing to join huddles during timeouts. LeBron kept his spirits up, cheering from the sidelines. But inside he was burning. Never in his career had he sat out crunch time of close games.

Team USA lost three times, twice in the qualifying rounds, and to Argentina in the semifinals. LeBron averaged only 5.4 points in 12.1 minutes per game. This was his first experience of a coach not believing he was among the top players on the team — a coach not showing confidence in LeBron to make big plays, or even be on the court when it mattered most. He was angry with Brown. (The next season, LeBron scored 41 points in his first game against Brown's Pistons.) He also wasn't sure he wanted to play in the Olympics, with some players who didn't take it that seriously, and a coach who was fearful of looking bad if the team failed.

■ ■

Meanwhile, USA Basketball, the body that selects the U.S. Olympic team, was under new leadership. Jerry Colangelo, the managing director of the men's senior national team, realized the world had made a statement on the court in several international competitions: Team USA was no longer a dominant basketball power. Especially if Team USA continued to approach these events by just throwing a team of stars together with a big-name coach and expecting them to win on sheer talent. Colangelo had to take a new approach, and he wanted LeBron to be the cornerstone of a team that he hoped would reclaim the gold medal in the 2008 Olympics.

Colangelo met with LeBron right after Christmas in 2005 when the Cavs were in Chicago. Convincing LeBron to sign on to the program was vital. He could be a magnet to attract other young stars. But Colangelo was asking a lot, a three-year commitment leading up to the 2008 Olympics. It was an effort to construct team chemistry, and for the players to know this was not just another All-Star game or casual summertime romp on the court. In the past, pro players wavered on their commitments up until June before the Olympics. Many players backed

**THE LEBRON FILE**
LeBron owns four international medals: a gold medal from the 2008 Olympics, a bronze medal from the 2004 Olympics, a gold medal from the 2007 FIBA Americas Championship, and a bronze medal from the 2006 FIBA World Championship.

out as the date approached. The three-year concept didn't appeal to some. Olympic veterans like Tim Duncan passed and so did Shaquille O'Neal.

LeBron told Colangelo that he was disillusioned by how he was treated in 2004, and how Brown alienated the young stars. There was some talk that LeBron, Carmelo Anthony and Dwyane Wade would perhaps skip playing for the national team. Entering the meeting, Colangelo was aware of this feeling. Bringing LeBron into the fold right away wouldn't only help convince others to accept the three-year deal but also signify a truly fresh start.

All three players were members of the 2003 draft. All had each other on cell phone speed dial. All felt a combination of competition and admiration for each other. And even in 2005, Colangelo believed LeBron had the strongest leadership gifts of the three — despite being the youngest. That's why he pursued LeBron first. If LeBron agreed, there was an excellent chance the others would follow.

When Duke Coach Mike Krzyzewski was hired to take over as coach of Team USA, LeBron was convinced the change would make the team better. In his first few years of high school, LeBron sometimes talked about attending Duke and playing for Krzyzewski. LeBron also was impressed when Krzyzewski assembled an excellent staff with Phoenix Suns coach Mike D'Antoni, Portland Trail Blazers coach Nate McMillan, and Syracuse coach Jim Boeheim.

When the team gathered for practice in the summer of 2006 in Las Vegas, the roster included veteran players such as Shane Battier and Antawn Jamison. Kobe Bryant wanted to play, but he was out with knee surgery. In the 2005–06 season, LeBron led the Cavs to 50 victories and a second-round spot in the playoffs. He also was second in the Most Valuable Player Award. With that momentum, the Team USA coaching staff was hoping LeBron would be one of the team leaders. They counted on his energy and upbeat personality to rub off on some of the other players in practice. But in his first days with the team LeBron seemed distracted. While he said he wanted a different approach to the Olympics, he was still stuck in the 2004 model where players went through the motions during the day, thinking about what they had planned for that evening. The coaches and even some of the players felt LeBron was going through the motions in drills. He wasn't showing much leadership when the team did its 5-on-5 work in practice. He often seemed indifferent in team meetings.

▬ ▬

Without Bryant, and with a new and mostly younger cast, the expectation was that LeBron would step up and grab at least some of the leadership. Krzyzewski had a few talks with LeBron, and the young star slowly improved in all areas, on and off the court. But that first training camp was generally a letdown, at least to the coaches who arrived with high expectations.

"LeBron was young and Coach K was feeling his way," said Jerry Colangelo. "They both had heard a lot about each other but didn't know each other. That first summer was important for them."

"It was a feeling-out process with Coach K and with all the players," said Mike D'Antoni. "It's why Colangelo wanted a three-year commitment, so that you can define [player] roles. The first time that you see it, everything was a little bit of a shock for everyone. We didn't get it totally right that first summer but we kept working and it solidified. We understood what LeBron could do. Coach K had a lot of talks [with LeBron], and he eventually just seized that moment. LeBron was one of the three guys who we had for all three summers. That ended up being huge for us, and huge for LeBron too because by the end he fully grasped it."

When Team USA went to Japan for the World Championships, they won their first six games easily. But in their first tough game, they were wiped out by Greece's pick-and-roll offense. The Greeks ran the same basic play time and time and time again without Team USA stopping it. Greece had several NBA draft picks on the team along with veteran point guard Theo Papaloukas, who was a well-known European star.

Krzyzewski never changed his defense, when a zone would have been the antidote. Another problem was that LeBron and the other leaders didn't show signs of stepping up to gather the team together in the crucial moments.

These events were the turning point for Krzyzewski, LeBron and many of the other players. After the loss to Greece, there was an off-day with no practice. Krzyzewski had a private meeting with LeBron, Anthony and Wade at the team hotel. He challenged them to recover to win the bronze medal game because it would set the tone for the next two summers. They were playing Argentina, who had won the 2004 Olympic gold medal. It turned out to be the first time there was a serious leadership statement from LeBron. During the meeting, he asked to be moved to point guard, where the team had been having trouble. That showed he knew what needed to be done — and was willing to do it, even if it meant him playing out of his natural position and perhaps sacrificing some scoring. LeBron went out and led a dominating win over Argentina at point guard, avenging the loss to Argentina in the 2004 Olympics. He had 22 points, nine rebounds and seven assists as Team USA won 96-81.

"When you are a superstar, you have a unique opportunity to be a leader. What you can do on the floor will inspire your teammates," said D'Antoni. "So what you try to do as a coach is present to the player what you think he can do for you. The opportunity was there for LeBron to become a great leader. He was already one of the best players on the planet. He eventually seized the moment. He bought into it and represented the United States."

> **THE LEBRON FILE**
> LeBron passed Brad Daugherty to become the Cavaliers' all-time leading scorer on March 21, 2008. He scored his 10,390th point by making a lay-up against the Toronto Raptors.

## MVP SEASON MOMENTS

For the first time in his career, in 2008–09, LeBron
was voted to the NBA's All-Defensive Team.

PLAIN DEALER PHOTOGRAPH | LISA DEJONG

A year after taking the bronze medal in the 2006 World Championships, Team USA had to play in the FIBA Americas Championships to earn a spot in the Olympics, at an event in Las Vegas. Now healthy again, Kobe Bryant joined Team USA for the first time in his career. And to help with the point guard issues, Colangelo convinced veteran Jason Kidd to join the team. Both additions ended up having a significant impact on LeBron. Kidd and LeBron knew each other, but were not close. A few months before, LeBron had knocked Kidd's New Jersey Nets out of the playoffs on the way to his first NBA Finals appearance. LeBron and Bryant had virtually no relationship. While they saw each other at All-Star Games and various summer events, and were also featured Nike pitchmen, they moved in opposite worlds. Bryant was much older. LeBron still had his high school buddies, and his NBA friends from the 2003 draft.

LeBron arrived in Las Vegas with a new sense of confidence after leading the Cavs to the 2007 Finals, which had ended only a month before. LeBron also had a new determination to improve after a poor showing in the Finals when the Spurs exposed his inconsistent mid-range jumper. LeBron had dedicated himself to upgrading his game, approaching this with more passion than at any previous point in his pro career.

In Kidd, LeBron saw an incredible leader, not just on the floor, but in huddles and team meetings. Kidd also put on a remarkable display of unselfishness during that FIBA Americas Tournament, going entire games without shooting the ball. He was also dedicated to the new system that the coaches wanted to play. Team USA started blowing everyone out and won easily to get the berth in China. Even Krzyzewski showed some growth. On the first possession of the tournament, the Americans came out in a zone defense.

But what really struck LeBron was Kidd's attitude. "He is one of the best point guards in the history of the game," LeBron said after that summer experience. "For me personally, it was definitely a good experience to watch how he put the team before himself and it carried over to everyone."

Then there was Bryant, whose impact on LeBron was just as profound. As is his nature, Bryant was serious about the task at hand, and his work ethic was nearly unrivaled by the other stars. Bryant was often the first player on the practice floor and the last player off. On the court, Bryant has a sharp edge to his personality, much like Michael Jordan. He is as demanding on his teammates as he is relentless to beat his opponent. But he pushes himself harder than anyone else. Bryant didn't have the same close relationships as Kidd and LeBron did with many of the Team USA players. But his intense focus was eye-opening for everyone. Soon, LeBron was following a similar practice regimen. Cavs assistant coach Chris Jent had flown in from Cleveland to put in time with LeBron on his shot, and they were spending more time in the gym than ever before. LeBron had two schedules going: his USA Basketball commitments and his own private workouts with Jent and others.

"Kobe served as an impetus for LeBron, whether LeBron knew that or not," said Jerry Colangelo. "Just by him being there, Kobe raised the bar for everyone — but especially LeBron. Over the last 40 years I've spent working in the NBA, I learned that sometimes players aren't totally aware of what they have left to give. LeBron had a lot more to give, and Kobe helped bring that out in him. When Kidd and Kobe got there, it helped considerably. They grew together and had a unique chemistry. Off the court they were friendly, but different. Kobe is more private and LeBron is more outgoing. But on the court they served as a constant challenge for each other."

LeBron never doubted he could blend his game with Bryant's.

"I'm probably the ultimate team player," he told the media covering Team USA. "I'll sacrifice whatever for the success of the team. Kobe is a great, great, great

**THE LEBRON FILE**
Before games, LeBron often eats fruit in the locker room, but sometimes he likes to eat chicken fingers.

player. It's not hard for me and Kobe to get along."

That summer, LeBron unveiled his new and more technically sound jumper — a nagging issue for years. He'd had a bad habit of fading backward on his shots. LeBron started making shots with stunning regularity, which took some by surprise. He'd made only 32 percent of his shots in the Finals just weeks before. During the 2007 tournament, LeBron shot a remarkable 62 percent on three-pointers by making 23 of 37. The FIBA three-point line is about a foot closer than in the NBA, but there was little doubt that LeBron's shooting had improved.

Something else was becoming apparent: Kidd had emerged as the soul of the team. He was driven to convince his teammates to surrender their egos for the larger goal of winning the gold. Bryant was the go-to player on the court, as he had been for every team he'd ever been on, the guy who takes the most important shot in the most critical situations. But LeBron was becoming the team's voice. His personality and mixture of skills, his willingness to learn and to concentrate upon making the offense work impressed his coaches and older teammates.

"I'm not sure I've ever seen a young man mature as quickly as he did," said Colangelo. "He took major, dramatic steps."

LeBron took his new shot with him to the 2007-08 NBA season with the Cavs. He set a career high by shooting 48 percent from the field, which helped him win his first scoring title, averaging 30 points per game. After missing it the year before, LeBron was voted back onto the first team, All-NBA. He also finished third in the MVP voting. It was LeBron's best personal season as a pro. And there was no doubt much of it was a carryover from the summer before.

When LeBron re-joined his Team USA teammates in Las Vegas in late June of 2008 to begin the final preparations for the Beijing Olympics, the coaching staff was amazed at the way LeBron conducted himself, compared with two years earlier when they first worked with him.

About his leadership on the team, LeBron told reporters, "I knew it had to come from someone. It doesn't matter how good individuals are, if you don't have a leader, it's not going to be right. I took that responsibility from day 1, saying I'm going to be the vocal leader."

After several meetings over 18 months with LeBron, Krzyzewski realized his young star really did embrace the leadership role.

"[When I first met him], I thought he was a great young player," Mike Krzyzewski told the media covering Team USA. "Now, he's a great player. You didn't know he was going to be a leader. He's a terrific leader. He's one of the best leaders I've been around."

The Duke coach allowed LeBron to lead the team in drills and speak to the team before some practices. He also spoke in huddles during games, along with taking aside a player just to encourage him or listen to what a teammate had on his mind.

Thinking back to the 2004 Olympics, four years later LeBron told reporters: "We didn't have a leader. We just weren't a good team. We got to the semifinals just because of our individual abilities. It's totally different now."

LeBron loved the "team first" approach, and the coaching staff noticed the difference in his attitude.

"He had become our quarterback," said Mike D'Antoni. "What is special about LeBron is he sees the game without any sort of selfishness. That's a winning vision. When you have a guy with that ability, he needs to communicate it. When you have that, it is easier to make a united team."

Nate McMillan, the assistant who led the defense, said, "His voice became a part of what we did. First, he has a very loud, deep voice that everyone could hear. He acted like the quarterback on defense. We'd put him back there and he'd help his teammates because he sees the floor so well with his size and with his knowledge of what is going on within the game."

It says a lot about LeBron that he ended up as the

**THE LEBRON FILE**
After games, LeBron often enjoys eating sushi and mixed fruit in the locker room.

triggerman of the offense for the 2008 team that finally won the gold medal. That roster included talented point guards in Chris Paul and Jason Kidd. But the coaches recalled LeBron's operating of the offense back in 2006 in the World Games in Japan when Team USA rallied to win the bronze medal.

The 6-foot-8 LeBron played point guard during parts of some games, then switched to power forward to help inside. The 2008 Team USA was somewhat "small," as Colangelo had tried to stack the team with tall wing defenders and good shooters to deal with the matchups they expected to face. That was why LeBron spent some time at power forward. D'Antoni designed numerous plays that put LeBron in the high post, where he would get the ball with good position, with the option to dribble, pull up, and shoot or pass. This proved devastating for the opposition, who always had problems knowing how many defenders should cover LeBron. He would continually find weaknesses in the defense. If he was double-covered, he passed to an open man for a lay-up. If a single, smaller defender tried to cover him, LeBron used his size to drive to the basket.

"You could put him anywhere on the floor and he'd be effective as a playmaker." marveled D'Antoni. He wasn't the point guard, but he pretty much became the point person for a lot of our players. He's one of the biggest and strongest players on the court."

Team USA coaches believed the team's depth and pure athletic talent — namely its speed and jumping ability — was reason to increase the tempo and play a pressing and aggressive style of defense. Olympic games are eight minutes shorter than 48-minute NBA games. Most of the players on Team USA usually played at least 35 minutes or more a night. So by substituting liberally to constantly have fresh players on the floor, they put their most physical effort into the defensive end of the court. Because he could cover every position on the floor, LeBron spent time guarding everyone from point guards to centers. He was the point man on the pressing defense, often defending the other team's best player — unless Bryant had that role. Then LeBron took the second-best scorer.

Team USA won the 2008 gold medal by defeating Spain, 118-107. Dwyane Wade led the team

with 27 points, Bryant added 20, while LeBron scored 14 and grabbed six rebounds.

"After 2004, we touched base with each other and said we wanted to make a commitment to be part of USA Basketball and try to accomplish something we've never done before — win a gold medal," said LeBron. "Once we came together and we put in our time and our hearts — we gave up our summers."

But those summers made LeBron a better player in the winter, especially in the 2008–09 season. Cavs Coach Mike Brown studied Team USA's games closely. He came to training camp in 2008 planning to increase LeBron's time at power forward. It created a series of so-called "small" lineups that led to big success for LeBron and the Cavs the next sea-

**LeBron bonded with his Team USA teammates, especially Jason Kidd and Chris Paul.**

son. The Olympic experience inspired LeBron to improve his defense during the NBA season. He consistently guarded the opposition's top wing scorer. He came from the weak side to block the shots of players defended by teammates. He was voted to the NBA All-Defensive Team for the first time.

"I'm just a better basketball player mentally, physically and emotionally," LeBron said after the Olympics.

He proved it with the Cavs in his MVP season.

"When he won the MVP, the entire USA Basketball family took great pride," said Colangelo. "There's a special bond between all of us. We cer-

tainly understand that all of these guys are valuable assets to their teams. Some see playing with us in the summer as a great risk. But I think what happens is players all come back from the experience better off than being left on their own."

That was certainly LeBron's perspective.

"Winning the gold medal was one of the most special moments in my life, it was a great accomplishment," LeBron said. "I came away knowing that I could be a leader on a team that had Dwyane Wade, Carmelo Anthony, Kobe Bryant and guys like Jason Kidd. Now I know I can be a leader on any team I'm on."

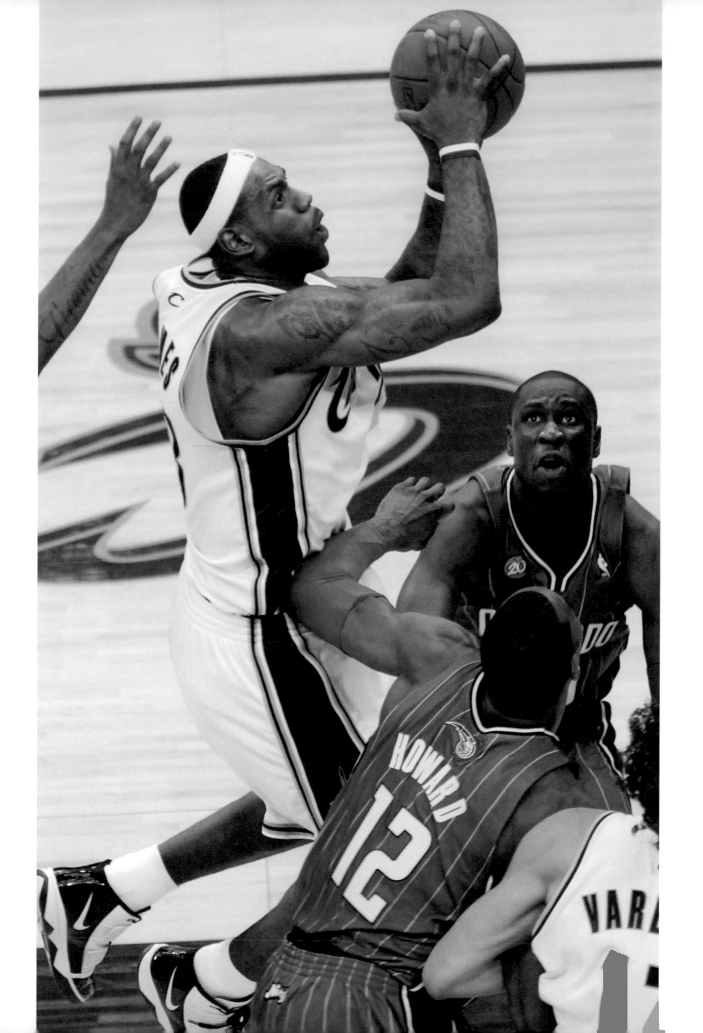

# Chapter 20. **Magic or Michael?**

In some games, LeBron James plays like Michael Jordan; in other games, he plays like Magic Johnson. This is not to make the claim that LeBron is as good as Jordan or Johnson, or that he will rival them even by the end of his career. But he is one of the few players in NBA history who can play like *either* of the two stars on any given night. He is one of the precious gifted few who can dominate a game with his passing one night, then own it with his scoring the next.

Magic Johnson was a 6-foot-9, 240-pound point guard in a power forward's body. The NBA had never seen such a physical specimen. He could set up in the low post near the basket and flip in a 10-foot hook shot, or grab 20 rebounds in a game, as he did a few times. But what made Johnson magic was his passing. His sense of team play. His knack of creating open shots for his teammates. He probably could have played in the NBA even if he had been only 6-foot because of his incredible ball-handling and passing skills. He could not, however, have averaged 30 points in a season. For his career, Johnson was a 19.5 scorer for the Lakers. His best season was 23.9. But for his career he averaged 11.2 assists, an NBA record. Johnson also averaged 7.2 rebounds, and won three MVP awards and five championship rings. The master of the triple-double (at least 10 rebounds, 10 assists and 10 points in a game), he had 138 in his career, a testimony to his all-around ability. The only player with more career triple-doubles is Oscar Robertson, with 181.

Then there's Jordan, perhaps the greatest basketball player ever.

Jordan won six championship rings, has an

**With his shot making ability and his awareness of the whole court, LeBron has developed into both a great scorer and a great passer.**

NBA record 10 season scoring titles and earned five MVP awards. He averaged an NBA record 30.12 points a game for his career, slightly more than even Chamberlain's 30.07. First and always, Jordan was a scorer. While Johnson had those 138 triple-doubles, Jordan had 28.

Where does Larry Bird fit? He seems to have had a more all-around game than Jordan, at least based on his 59 triple-doubles. Bird won three championship rings, three MVP awards. His career averages are terrific: 24.3 points, 10.0 rebounds and 6.3 assists. But unless you are from Boston, or bleed Celtic green, Johnson still has to be considered a better all-around player than Bird. Not by much, but his five titles (compared to three for Bird), seem to give him the edge — especially since both had Hall of Famers on their teams. Neither had to carry the same load as Jordan, who had as a teammate one great player in Scottie Pippen, but mostly role players after that on his six championship teams.

Why even bring LeBron into this discussion?

Because he won his first MVP award at the age of 24. Most players don't peak until their late 20s. Johnson and Bird were not awarded their first MVPs until they were 27. Jordan? His came at 25.

By the age of 24, LeBron had 24 triple-doubles, with four more in the playoffs, compared to two for Jordan.

PLAIN DEALER PHOTOGRAPH | JOHN KUNTZ

What about Kobe Bryant? He has won only one MVP award, that being in 2008 at the age of 29. More importantly, the guy doesn't pass — a career average of 4.6 assists. Certainly not an embarrassing total, but Jordan is at 5.3. Bird was 6.3 assists from his forward spot. LeBron, by the end of his sixth season had a career average of 6.7 assists.

For Bryant, the numbers remain at 25.1 points, 5.3 rebounds and those 4.6 assists. There is a sense that Bryant often is a "bailout passer," meaning he gives up the ball only when he's in trouble — being double- or tripled-teamed. Nearly every time he catches the ball, the first thing that crosses his mind is "shoot it."

What makes LeBron different is he can do everything, and is doing it at a younger age than nearly anyone has done it before. He also is doing it at a historic pace.

Consider the following:

February 9, 2004: LeBron became the youngest player in NBA history to score 1,000 points in a career. He later became the youngest player to reach the 5,000 and 10,000 points marks.

March 27, 2004: LeBron became the youngest player in NBA history to score 40 points in a game when he scorched the nets against New Jersey for 41 points.

January 20, 2005: LeBron became the youngest player in NBA history to record a triple-double: 27 points, 11 rebounds and 10 assists against Portland.

March 20, 2005: LeBron became the youngest player in NBA history to score 50 points when he threw in 54 points in a game at Toronto.

The list of LeBron being the youngest to ... never seems to end.

In 2007–08, he led the NBA in scoring, averaging 30 points per game. But he also averaged 7.9 rebounds and 7.2 assists. The only other players ever to average at least 30 points, seven rebounds and seven assists in a season were Robertson and Jordan.

"That's like shooting fish in a barrel [for LeBron]," said New York Knicks Head Coach Mike D'Antoni, who was an assistant coach with Team USA when they won the 2008 Olympic gold medal. He meant LeBron can score 40 or more points when his team needs it. Or he can pass off for a dozen assists.

Or as Olympic coach Mike Krzyzewski wrote in his book, "The Gold Standard": "LeBron would be our starter at point guard. This position is typically associated with the most coach-to-player communication in basketball. So by doing this, I was sending a message. LeBron James was going to be my leader on the court."

The coaching staff put LeBron in that role, not Kobe Bryant, Dwyane Wade or any of the other stars. They knew he could be their Magic Johnson, who had played the lead role on the 1992 Olympic Dream Team. Jordan and Bird also were on that team, but it belonged to Johnson. Just as the 2008 team seemed to be owned by LeBron, even when he wasn't the leading scorer.

For a superstar, being willing to fill whatever role is necessary to win does not come naturally. That's why Phil Jackson imposed a share-the-ball offense play called the Triangle Offense when he coached Jordan in Chicago.

In his book, "Sacred Hoops," written with Hugh Delehanty, Jackson characterized the modern NBA this way: "Today's players have a dazzling array of individual moves, most of which they've learned from coaches who encourage 1-on-1 play. In an effort to become 'stars,' young players will do almost anything to draw attention to themselves, to say, 'This is me' with the ball, rather than share the limelight with others."

He mentioned how former Bulls coach Doug Collins looked at Jordan averaging 37 points in 1985-86, and designed "dozens of plays" to get the ball to Jordan's teammates so they'd feel confident to shoot. But too often, they found it easier to throw the ball to Jordan and watch him take on the world. Then Collins moved Jordan to point guard, hoping that would create more ball movement. Jordan still averaged 32.5 points and there were a few more shots for his teammates.

"The problem with making Jordan a point guard, as I saw it, was it didn't address the real problem," wrote Jackson. "The prevalent style of offense in the NBA reinforced a self-centered approach to the game."

Jackson's use of the Triangle, created by basketball coach Tex Winter, was designed to change the entire mindset of every player, not just have a star change positions. But only Jackson has been able to make the offense play work in the NBA. A few other coaches tried it, but the players rebelled. They preferred one-on-one basketball, or the basic two-man, pick-and-roll play. Jackson was able to convince Jordan to buy into it — at least for the first three quarters of the game. In the fourth quarter, Jordan and the Bulls often reverted to the star dominating the ball.

Question: Who immediately comes to mind as the greatest scorer in NBA history?

Answer: Most fans and basketball experts would name Michael Jordan, with his all-time record 31.12 scoring average.

Question: Who is the greatest passer in NBA history?

Answer: Most would probably name Johnson, with his all time-record average of 11.2 assists.

Question: What player now can come closest to playing as those two stars did in their primes?

Answer: It would have to be LeBron.

Question: Why say that?

Answer: Because LeBron is capable of having huge, Jordanesque scoring games. He also has games where he can rack up the assists like Magic.

Question: Do you have proof?

Answer: Let's look at a three-day, two-game span from May 31-June 2, 2007. We are talking the Eastern Conference Finals. We are talking about Game 5 in Detroit, where LeBron led the Cavs to a 109-107 double-overtime victory. We are talking about LeBron scoring 48, including the Cavs last 25 points of the game. It truly was a Jordan-like performance. But two days later in Game 6 at Cleveland, he took only 11 shots, scoring 20 points. He had a playoff career-high 14 rebounds and eight as-

> **THE LEBRON FILE**
> LeBron is one of four players in NBA history to lead their team in all five major statistical categories (total points, total rebounds, total assists, total blocks and total steals) in a season. He did it in the 2008–09 season. The others were Dave Cowens with the Boston Celtics in 1977–78, Scottie Pippen with the Chicago Bulls in 1994–95 and Kevin Garnett with the Minnesota Timberwolves in 2002–03.

sists as the Cavs crushed the Pistons 98-82 to win the first conference title in franchise history.

What LeBron did in the two biggest games of his career was this: one night, he played like Michael Jordan with the 48 points. The next game, he knew that the Pistons would be firing on all cylinders to stop him, so he played like Magic Johnson, setting up his teammates for shots, and pounding the boards for 14 rebounds.

"You can put LeBron anywhere on the floor and he'd be effective as a playmaker," said Mike D'Antoni. "We wanted him in position where he could make a lot of plays ... but he's also one of the biggest and strongest players on the court. He has those Magic Johnson qualities."

Yet when former Cavaliers General Manager Wayne Embry watches LeBron, he flashes back to another No. 23 — Jordan.

In that Game 5 victory, LeBron scored outside and inside. He scored with his left hand, and his right hand. He also had seven assists in a game where his team only had 13. Yes, LeBron had seven assists, the other Cavs had six. That means that nearly all of LeBron's 18 field goals were the result of him taking the ball and taking on the best Detroit had to offer. It was the kind of game that Jordan often produced early in his career when he was trying to carry his young Bulls deep into the playoffs.

No player in NBA postseason history had ever finished a game with his team's final 25 points. Not even Jordan or Chamberlain, the two greatest scorers in NBA history. And the fact that this was an Eastern Conference playoff game makes it far more significant than just another March night in the NBA when several NBA teams are yawning on defense and dreaming of what they will do with their summer vacation. LeBron seemed to be talking about that when he said, "I made a lot of good moves and was able to finish. It wasn't like they just

**LeBron helped prove himself as a clutch player in 2007 with his creative layup to give the Cavs a Game 5 victory over the Detroit Pistons in the Eastern Conference Finals.**

opened up the lane and let me move through there."

A frustrated Detroit coach Flip Saunders said his team "wanted to get the ball out of LeBron's hands," but they could not find a way to do it. How often did Cavs fans hear that same type of comment from Cleveland coaches frustrated at not being able to stop Jordan in the clutch?

Great players can find a way to get off a shot in almost any circumstance.

In the 2009 playoffs, Orlando Coach Stan Van Gundy was overwhelmed at how LeBron drove the ball right into 7-foot Dwight Howard, the center who was voted the NBA Defensive Player of the Year: "LeBron goes right at his chin and nose, gets hit — and still scores. He's the best finisher in the game. He's not afraid to challenge anyone."

In Game 3, LeBron was more Jordan than Magic, with 32 points, nine rebounds and nine assists in an 88-82 victory. In Game 4, it was a little of both. LeBron finished with 25 points, but scored 14 in the fourth quarter. But he also had 11 assists and seven rebounds in the 91-87 victory. In order to win Game 5 of that Detroit series, the Cavs needed 48 points from LeBron in a Jordan-type performance.

What would he do in Game 6?

The spirit of Magic Johnson showed up.

LeBron knew the Pistons would send two, three, even four defenders at him on some plays. He knew that rookie point guard Daniel Gibson — who, in 2007, reminded LeBron of his old high school teammate Dru Joyce III — would be open. He knew that Gibson was starting to shoot the ball well with confidence. He knew that his passing could win this game, even more than his scoring.

LeBron was willing to make himself a decoy, setting up Gibson and others for shots. The result was a stunning 98-82 victory over Detroit, clinching the Cavs' first trip to the NBA Finals. LeBron attempted only five shots from the field in the first three quarters. For the game, he took only 11 shots, but scored 20 points. He had 14 rebounds, eight assists, and made sure the offense flowed. He kept drawing defenders like bees to honey, then delivering perfect passes to Gibson — who made shot, after shot, after shot. Gibson scored a career-high 31 points in that game. He was 5-of-5 on three-pointers. LeBron kept telling him, "If you are open, don't hesitate, shoot it."

And Gibson did.

Watching the game was Dru Joyce III.

"I could see [Gibson] getting that feeling," he said. "His feet were set. His shoulders were square. He knew LeBron would get him the ball. When they start to go in, you are focused on every shot. The rim is wider. The game is slower. It's like you are playing in your backyard."

LeBron later said the game reminded him of St. Vincent-St. Mary's first state title in the LeBron Era. That was in 2000, when the Irish defeated Greeneview, 73-55. Joyce III didn't even start that game, but Irish Coach Keith Dambrot put him in early to bring some spark to the team. Joyce III was only 5-foot-2 with shorts seemingly hanging down to his ankles. It was as if Dambrot had inserted a fourth-grader in the game, at least to the fans who had not seen the Irish before. But Joyce made his first shot from three-point range. And his second. And his third. And his fourth. And his fifth. And his sixth. And his seventh. And then the game was over.

In 10 minutes, Joyce III scored 21 points on 7-of-7 from the field, all three-pointers. In that game, LeBron was content to pass. He obviously was hot, making 10-of-12 shots for 25 points. But it was

even more important for him to make sure that Joyce III got the ball. So LeBron snared nine rebounds, dishing out five assists.

"Watching Gibson [in Game 6 of the 2007 Eastern Conference Finals] was a lot like seeing Little Dru in that state title game," said Dambrot. "You could sense what was coming, that Gibson was hot, and LeBron would keep setting him up. You can talk about him scoring 48 points, but LeBron is happier when he's feeding Gibson and the other guys."

Or as Dru Joyce II said, "Keith [Dambrot] always drilled into the players to throw the extra pass. That's how [Little] Dru got those open looks in the championship game. It's what happened with Gibson [in 2007]. Move the ball. LeBron loves to do that."

Dambrot added, "Everybody thought LeBron was going to win that game. But there's LeBron doing the right thing, passing to this 92-pound freshman. Years from now, people will talk about LeBron in the tournament. Then someone will mention that little kid making all the three-pointers. He's part of the folklore."

Those who have coached LeBron — from Joyce II to Dambrot in summer leagues and high school, to Paul Silas and Mike Brown with the Cavs, to LeBron's Olympic coaches — all insist LeBron can play any style, and is willing to do so.

"When I first visualized LeBron playing in the NBA, I saw him more as Magic than Michael," said Dambrot. "I thought he was the best passer I'd ever seen. I thought he'd lead the league in assists. Then he developed into this scoring maniac. That really is not his personality. He is a combination of Magic and Michael. He had to go in the scoring direction in his first years with the Cavs because he didn't have all the pieces [talented teammates] to become Magic Johnson. So he became more Michael Jordan. But he's one of the few players who can be both, Magic or Michael. And that is a big part of what makes him great."

**THE LEBRON FILE**
LeBron set a Cavaliers franchise record for minutes played in a single season with 3,388 during the 2004–05 season.

# Chapter 21. **A Leader**

## "LeBron allows me to coach him."

That's what Mike Brown said not long after becoming head coach of the Cleveland Cavaliers in the summer of 2005

Many fans were surprised. It sounded as if LeBron were in charge, telling Brown what to do. But Brown was just describing reality in the NBA. Stars and coaches work together. If they don't, it's usually the coach who loses. Owners and general managers tend to side with the star, because it's a lot easier to find a new coach than it is another star.

San Antonio coach Gregg Popovich is considered a disciplinarian. He is a product of the Air Force Academy, a guy who demands that his team play defense, act and dress like gentlemen in public and treat each other with respect.

But even Popovich says, "Tim Duncan allows me to coach him."

Duncan is the Spurs star center, a rather mild-mannered product of Wake Forest University. Once Duncan joined Popovich and the Spurs, four NBA titles followed. Mike Brown was an assistant coach with the Spurs when they won the 2003 title. Much of what Brown does in terms of the accent on defense comes from his San Antonio days. But he also watched how Popovich dealt with stars such as David Robinson, Tony Parker and Duncan — and that influenced his approach to LeBron.

"I learned from Pop [Popovich] that the best way to coach is to give the players some ownership over the decisions you make," said Brown.

Although Mike Brown's name was on a list of four possible coaches for the Cavs submitted by fu-

**Over four years, LeBron and coach Mike Brown have grown together by learning from each other.**

ture General Manager Danny Ferry to team owner Dan Gilbert, Ferry himself had not yet been hired to run the Cavs. Gilbert was still interviewing coaching candidates. Some were available and wanted the job. That group included Eric Musselman and Flip Saunders. He also spoke with several career assistants, and touched base with Hall of Fame coaches Phil Jackson and Larry Brown, although they were consulted as advisors rather than candidates.

Gilbert spent 45 minutes with Mike Brown and came away convinced that he should be the next head coach. The Cavs owner called it "the best interview that I've ever had with anyone."

The hiring was a gamble. Brown had never played in the NBA. He had never been a head coach at any level. Yes, he had been an assistant at Indiana, Denver, Washington and San Antonio, but that's far different from being the head coach, making the quick in-game decisions and dealing with off-court issues such as discipline, or players unhappy with their court time or contracts, or second-guessing from the media. While he could talk a great game about how defense wins titles, as far as how to communicate with players and how to develop LeBron, there was no way to know if Brown could actually do it. Or just as critical, would LeBron buy the style of coaching that Brown was selling, as LeBron had no prior relationship with Brown.

In their first meeting, Brown went to the amusement park Cedar Point with LeBron. Brown tried to do bonding sessions with several of his players. The trip to the amusement park was LeBron's idea. Brown wasn't exactly comfortable there: Le-Bron was drawing a lot of attention as he walked around the Northwestern Ohio park. But LeBron wanted to meet with the coach in a relaxed atmosphere, and maybe have a little fun on some rides, too. While LeBron had already had two seasons as a pro and been an All-Star, he still was only 20 years old at this first meeting.

Just as LeBron had done with his first pro coach, Paul Silas, LeBron did some checking on Brown. He talked to some members of the Indiana Pacers, Brown's last coaching stop. Pacers star Jermaine O'Neal raved about Brown to LeBron, insisting the Cavs had made an excellent choice. LeBron knew the new general manager, Danny Ferry. LeBron had watched Ferry play for the Cavs, and they had met a few times. Ferry was an assistant general manager in San Antonio before coming to Cleveland — and he had known Brown well from their days together with the Spurs.

"The first thing the Cavs and LeBron needed was stability," said Ferry. "You establish that by getting the right coach, the right players and doing things the right way. You stick with it, and give the coach time to grow."

Ferry mentions the recent success of San Antonio, the Lakers and Utah — teams that rarely change coaches and general managers. He believes they are contenders every year not only because they have stars, but because they have coaches with clear philosophies, and that permits the front offices to know what kind of players must be acquired to make the team work. In Utah, coach Jerry Sloan likes players who love to defend. So does Gregg Popovich, but the Spurs coach also needs a couple of veterans who can come off the bench and make long-range shots — creating room for Tim Duncan to operate inside. The Lakers are the only team running the Triangle

**Brown's biggest influence on LeBron has been to make him a better defensive player.**

Offense, which stresses the need for players to keep moving when they don't have the ball.

Ferry and Brown were primarily influenced by their San Antonio experience. They saw how Popovich really listened when he had discussions with players. They watched him implement some ideas from the players. Despite Popovich's well-deserved reputation as a disciplinarian, there was a side of him that knew players sometimes had good ideas — and also, if a coach can come up with concepts in concert with his key players, then it is much easier to sell to the entire team. The coach has advocates in the dressing room in players who are respected by the rest of the team.

Hall of Fame coach Chuck Daly turned to Isiah Thomas, Bill Laimbeer and Rick Mahorn before making any major coaching decisions. He had them draw up rules for conduct on the road regarding curfews, dress codes, etc. Daly said the rules designed by the players were stricter than what he had in mind for the team. During one of the Detroit Pistons championship drives, the entire team voted not to drink during the playoffs — not even a casual beer. Had Daly tried to enforce

PLAIN DEALER PHOTOGRAPH | ROADELL HICKMAN

that rule without the support of his team captains, there would have been a revolt. Instead, the three captains suggested it, and Daly told them to get the rest of the team on board — which they did.

"In this league, a good coach has to have enough self-confidence to allow some players a strong voice," said Danny Ferry. "Even when he was young, LeBron had the leadership ability you want."

At the age of 20, LeBron was named team captain not long after Brown was hired in the summer of 2005. It was a learning process for both of them. No matter how much experience an assistant coach has, it really is up to the head coach to set the tone. Brown had strong coaches in Popovich and Indiana's Rick Carlise to back him up before he came to the Cavs. Now, Brown was in charge.

"LeBron could be a leader at such a young age because he had high character and a great work ethic," said Brown. "He also has a high basketball IQ. What he needed was an organization that was stable, and where there were not a lot of distractions."

From the moment he was hired, Brown stressed the need for defense. He also wanted an outside shooter to pressure the opposing defenses, so LeBron would not always be double-, even triple-teamed. It was the basic basketball cake baked by the Spurs, but Brown and Ferry added their own style of frosting.

That first season together (2005-06), the Cavs got off to a 7-2 start and finished with a 50-32 record, the best in LeBron's three seasons. It also was the first time LeBron's team made the playoffs. The accent on defense also helped carry the Cavs to the second round of the playoffs, where they lost to Detroit in Game 7 on the Pistons' home floor.

It was during Brown's second season in 2006-07 that his first real coaching crisis came. The team was struggling to score: LeBron was feeling enormous pressure to score, and teammates such as Larry Hughes and Donyell Marshall were in

> **THE LEBRON FILE**
> LeBron got his first triple double on Jan. 15, 2005 in Portland, when he had 27 points, 11 rebounds and 10 assists. He got his second just two nights later in a game at Golden State.

shooting slumps. The initial high that came from a team with few expectations the season before, and then won 50 games to advance to the second round of the playoffs — that thrill was gone. Now, the Cavs were supposed to be one of the elite teams in the league. But LeBron was wondering if all the defense demands were draining too much energy, hurting his offense. It was Hughes who first raised that question with the media, criticizing the offense for being too structured, too slow-paced. LeBron seconded the opinion, unhappy the team couldn't run more because of the focus on ball control and defense.

Brown responded by calling a meeting with LeBron and Hughes. He listened to them, wanting to know what they considered to be their major concern. The players believed the coaching staff was preventing them from fastbreaking and running some freelance offense. Too many set plays were being called from the bench.

Rather than feeling threatened by this, Brown quickly sensed a compromise could be reached. The coaches wanted to keep up the high standards on defense. To them, the offense was not quite as important. The players were not really debating the value of defense; they just wanted more freedom on offense. Brown said if the players were willing to give a dedicated effort on the defensive end, then they could run more and play offense with freedom to drive the ball up the court. The Cavs came together as a team in the second half and shockingly put together a drive to the Eastern Conference championship for the first time in franchise history. Although they eventually were swept in the 2007 Finals by the Spurs, Brown had established himself as a head coach, and LeBron had cemented his role as team captain with the strategic compromise.

"I make all the final decisions," said Brown. "But a coach has to work to communicate with the players."

If that breaks down, someone loses their job — usually the coach.

Early in the career of Magic Johnson, the Lakers star believed coach Paul Westhead was too controlling when it came to the offense. Westhead was fired less than two years after winning an NBA championship. Pat Riley took over, and bonded with Johnson to develop what became the Lakers' freewheeling "Showtime offense." Riley is now a Hall of Fame coach, and his relationship with Magic Johnson and Kareem Abdul-Jabbar had a lot to do with that. Later in his career, Riley became a defensive coach, building teams in New York around physical center Patrick Ewing. He then went to Miami and won a title with Shaquille O'Neal and Dwyane Wade. Like Popovich, Riley is known for having a disciplined team — yet, his stars have also backed and appreciated him.

But a different story occurred in Orlando, where young star Penny Hardaway clashed with Coach Brian Hill. Hardaway called a players-only meeting, asking teammates if they wanted to continue to play for Hill, or to get a new coach. The players voted against Hill. Hardaway told the front office of the vote, and Hill was fired.

"You need your top guy with you," said Brown. "If it comes down to LeBron and me, only three people will pick me: my mother, my father and my wife."

Brown laughed that even his kids would probably back LeBron.

"I think everyone else would get rid of me," he said.

The power of the players in the NBA is the reason why the average pro coach lasts slightly longer than three years with one team.

In Brown's third season, 2007-08, the Cavs had injuries and other problems. A few players, including Larry Hughes, were not happy. Fans were highly critical of Brown's offense. While LeBron himself was not critical of his coach, he was hardly pleased with how the team was playing. Rather than fire Brown, Ferry made a major trade — shipping Hughes, Donyell Marshall and others for two mature veterans, Ben Wallace and Joe Smith. They also added Delonte West, an unselfish guard who likes to

defend. Both the trade and the new teammates revived LeBron. While the Cavs lost to Boston in the second round of the playoffs, it was clear the team was supporting Brown. LeBron backed his coach, but pushed the front office to add more talent.

"We've dealt with some things that have gone the right way and times when things have gone the wrong way," said LeBron. "He's given me responsibility and helped me become a leader of the team. He's always been very open with me. It helped us learn to trust in each other. That is important in a coach-player relationship."

Former Cavs star-turned-broadcaster Austin Carr has watched the relationship between LeBron and Brown mature.

"The first thing is, the coach has to know what he is talking about," said Carr. "Even if the coach is a good guy and the players like him — there will be problems if the system is flawed, if the coach doesn't adjust to the talent. Mike was able to convince LeBron and the others that the only way to get to the Promised Land and a title is with defense, and they had some success doing that right away."

LeBron appreciates the stability that the Cavs have in place with Brown.

"Mike Brown knows me and I know him," LeBron said. "We both know the system like our kids. We have a great comfort level with each other that we've built over the years."

Carr said it was clear to the players that Ferry and Brown not only were on the same page in terms of how the team should operate, but they seemed to say the same sentences. This is important, because if the players sense a division between the general manager and coach — the players will go over the head of the coach to the front office with their complaints. That often leads to the coach being fired. But if there is a problem with a player, Ferry and Brown work together with the player to resolve it.

"LeBron likes to be coached, and he loves to win," said Carr. "He's not like some stars, who worry about their scoring averages. He wants to play the

**THE LEBRON FILE**
LeBron has never worn glasses, but he had Lasik surgery on both eyes before the 2007 season. It was performed in California by a doctor used by numerous Hollywood celebrities.

**Thanks in part to LeBron's performance on the court and support in the locker room, Mike Brown was named NBA Coach of the Year in 2009.**

game the right way, and that helps his coach."

In the summer of 2008, the Cavs made a huge deal by adding Mo Williams, who later became an All-Star guard. They won an NBA-best 66 regular-season games, then lost to Orlando in the Eastern Conference Finals.

During the playoffs, LeBron was named the MVP, and he brought the entire team on stage when he accepted the award. He also praised Brown and the coaching staff.

"Our relationship has grown tremendously," LeBron said. "It happens when you go through the seasons and the playoff wars and things like that. I've grown as a player with him and he's grown as a coach on that path."

Brown agrees: "LeBron has grown by leaps and bounds in the time we've been together. It's an honor to coach him when he won his first MVP Award. He puts in so much work, especially on his own time, because he's so hungry to be the best and it propels him."

Then Brown hit on his favorite theme — defense.

"LeBron has grown so much as a team defender," the coach said. "He's developed a great feel for not only his job but what everyone else on the court should be doing, and he helps. He's such an amazing communicator out on the court. He has a certain confidence in what he's doing because he's been in this system. He helps us as coaches in that way. He's really like a quarterback for us out there on the floor."

Then there's LeBron the person.

"As a leader, he's all-world for us," said Brown. "That comes from spending so much time in that role and he's also developed it with his dealings away from us. [His experience] with Team USA and being the captain of that team has carried over [to the Cavaliers]. Plus, all those business endeavors have taught him how to manage complex situations and different personalities. He's grown as much in that aspect than in any other, truly. Not only is he becoming one of the greatest players ever, but he's got a chance to become one of the greatest leaders ever."

## Chapter 22. **In the Clutch**

To make a game-winning shot, you have to be willing to take the shot.

Sounds obvious, but not everyone on the court wants that final, pressurized last shot. If you're LeBron James and you attempt a shot in the final few seconds of a game with your team behind, you know the other team is setting its defense to stop you. The other team wants anyone but you to take the shot. The other team has a tremendous advantage because when only a few seconds remain, you have very few options.

Catch a pass. Take a shot. Maybe pray a bit.

That's it.

If you miss, your critics won't remember all the shots Michael Jordan banged off the rim as the buzzer blared. Or the times that Kobe Bryant failed to connect in the clutch. Or the times that last-shot attempts by Larry Bird rimmed out. Or when a Kareem Abdul-Jabbar skyhook shot sliced off the front of the rim.

When you're LeBron James, you still remember one last-second shot — an off-balance 12-foot-

**Beating the buzzer in Game 2 of the 2009 Eastern Conference Finals, "LeShot" was one of the greatest in NBA history.**

PLAIN DEALER PHOTOGRAPH | JOHN KUNTZ

er that bounced around the rim and rolled off with the final horn when you were a sophomore in high school. Had the shot been true, your St. Vincent-St. Mary team would have upset Oak Hill Academy, the top-ranked high school team in the country in 2001. But you missed. It still bothers you, because you also missed two free throws and a wide-open jumper from the foul line in the final minute. Your team lost 79-78, a game where you scored 33 points but believed you let your team down.

You remember that shot you missed in the summer of 1998, way back in your junior-high years. Had it gone in, you would have given your Akron Shooting Stars a huge upset victory over a team of all-stars from California in a national AAU tournament.

You remember the 2005–2006 NBA season. There was an early season game in Charlotte. The Cavs had won the night before in San Antonio — a key win, the first victory there in 17 years. You seemed weary that next night in Charlotte, but the Bobcats were dreadful. The Cavs blew a lead late and the game was tied. For the first time all season (it was just the fourth game) they ran a play called "Flat." It was a 1-4 setup. It's the kind of play a coach designs for a star player. You were the "1", the man with the ball at the top of the key. Your four teammates spread out on the wings and corners, leaving the middle wide open for you to drive to the basket — if you can beat your man with your dribble. And you believe you can get past anyone. Only on this night, your concentration was poor, your sense of the 24-second clock is off. You turned and dribbled and backed down Matt Carroll, a lanky guard. You could have overpowered Carroll with just a normal effort. But you wasted time, you didn't get to the rim — and finally flung up an off-balance air ball. The Cavs then lost in overtime. It was a low moment. The media ripped you for how you handled that possession.

But there was a game in April of 2006 at Oklahoma City. The Cavs were fighting for home-court advantage in the playoffs. The Hornets, with a young Chris Paul, were hustling to make the playoffs. The Cavs ran Flat. You drove, faked a pass and

then pulled up from 18 feet and hit the shot with one second left to win the game. It wasn't technically a "buzzer beater," but it was your first game-winning shot in the final seconds in the NBA.

It also helped your confidence. In the 2006 playoffs, the Cavs made three shots in the last 10 seconds to win games against the Washington Wizards. You delivered two of those, both with brute force. One shot was in Game 3 in Washington, when you drove the ball to the rim. You were fouled by Michael Ruffin (no call), but you banked it home anyway. Then in Game 5 (both games broke ties in the series) you shook Antawn Jamison on a risky

**Sasha Pavlovic grabs LeBron in celebration as the crowd explodes following the buzzer beater.**

drive to the basket because it seemed you were about to step out of bounds on the baseline. But somehow, you got to the rim and scored again. The other game was won by a Damon Jones jumper.

You remember Game 1 of the 2007 playoffs, the second round, in Detroit, where you passed the ball to a wide-open Donyell Marshall, who missed an open jumper from the corner. You were criticized for not taking the shot, despite the fact that the corner was Marshall's favorite spot to shoot from.

In Game 2 you forced up a medium-range jumper against two defenders. You were definitely bumped, but no foul was called. And the shot banged off the rim.

Two tight games in the playoff spotlight in Detroit. Once, you passed and the Cavs lost. Once, you shot and the Cavs lost. Both times, critics said you were wrong. You weren't Michael. You weren't Kobe. You didn't produce under pressure.

Every future MVP reaches the point where he has to come to terms with the pressure of taking the last shot. It's not just the miss that hurts, it's the reaction after. It's walking into a dressing room, feeling that you let down your coaches and teammates. That pressure has been enough to turn confident players timid, to prevent them from going from good to great. You can tell yourself that when you miss the final shot and your team loses, it's not the end of the world. No one died. You still have your health. You still have more money than you can ever spend. You still have your family and friends. You still have everything that really is important.

Only inside, you don't feel that way.

Especially if you are LeBron James, and you want to please people — want them to know that you can be counted upon to deliver for them when it means the most.

When you're LeBron James, and deep down you know that eventually you should be the most valuable player of the greatest basketball league in the world, you have to start making these shots. And you have to be mentally strong enough to deal with missing these big shots. You need a little Michael Jordan in your heart every time the clock ticks, ticks, ticks down to the final, precious seconds in a tight game.

Jordan once said, in a TV commercial, "I've missed 9,000 shots in my career. I've lost almost 300 games … 26 times I've been trusted to take the game-winning shot and missed. I've failed over and over again in my life … but I've never been afraid to fail."

Jordan's first big shot was in his freshman year at North Carolina, giving the Tar Heels the national title. But the shot for which he is best known, the one that has been branded into the memory of Cleveland sports fans and dubbed simply "The Shot," happened May 7, 1989, at the old Coliseum in Richfield, Ohio. LeBron was five years old at the time, so he didn't actually see it happen. But ever since he began paying attention to pro sports, LeBron heard about Jordan's jumper at the foul line over the Cavs' Craig Ehlo. He had seen that replay, over and over — featured in a Jordan highlight

> **THE LEBRON FILE**
> LeBron started his playoff career with 19 consecutive 20-point games. The only player with more was Kareem Abdul-Jabbar, with 27. LeBron's streak ended against the New Jersey Nets.

package or on a Cleveland sports lowlights review. He knows the Cavs lost that game, 101-100, and that shot knocked them out of the playoffs.

But few people recall that the Cavs had won the previous game in Chicago, 108-105 in overtime, when Jordan missed a couple of clutch free throws on his own court.

In the Chicago huddle, Coach Doug Collins had his own version of Flat. He told the team, "Get the ball to Michael and everyone else get out of the way."

No worries about what had happened in the previous game, but Chicago fans were very aware of the Bulls' No. 23 failing in the clutch. As Jordan's shot dropped at the buzzer, Bulls broadcaster Jim Durham said: "Inbounds pass comes in to Jordan. Here's Michael at the foul line … the shot on Ehlo … GOOD! The Bulls win! They win! Superman was Superman and no one is going to talk about that missed free throw in Game 4 now!"

LeBron was gaining that same courage on the court.

In the 2008–2009 season, there was a road game against the Golden State Warriors. The Cavs were playing poorly. It looked like it would be a loss when suddenly LeBron took a side out-of-bounds possession, got the shot up just ahead of the buzzer, and made it.

Most fans don't realize it, but the odds are drastically against you when shooting in the final 24 seconds of a close game, when the teams are within two points of each other. In an excellent article on the Web site 82games.com, writer Roland Beech determined that about 30 percent of those shots go in.

It's generally assumed that Kobe Bryant is a tremendous clutch player. That's true. But from 2003–09, he was 14-of-56 (25 percent) in those "game winning shots."

As Beech wrote, "We're not Kobe haters by any

**The Cavs often rely on James to win games in the clutch, and he has often carried the load.**

means and I will readily give him his due as one of the best NBA players (note however, I didn't say the best) but he certainly has an overblown reputation when it comes to the clutch shot: people remember the ones he hits, but not the ones he misses, and heck, you think a 56 FGA-to-1 assist ratio might be part of the problem?"

Bryant shoots nearly every time in that situation, and it's not always the best decision. LeBron has delivered six assists to win games. He also came up 17-of-50 (34 percent) from the field. That is above average. LeBron began his pro career at 4-of-19 in his first three seasons. That means he was 13-of-31 (42 percent) as he's gained experience.

"I never looked at the consequences of missing a big shot … when you think about the consequences, you always think of a negative result," Jordan said after he retired.

Lakers Hall of Fame Coach Phil Jackson said a player in those situations needs "to step into the moment." Just play that game, that day, that possession. Don't try to drive with one eye in the rear-view mirror, because you'll miss an opening, and in the end, you'll probably crash.

LeBron learned all this in his six years as a pro building up to his MVP season.

It was on May 22, 2009, slightly more than 20 years after Jordan's shot.

When the ball came off the fingertips of LeBron's huge right hand, for a second, it looked good, real good.

"But for me, a second is a long time," LeBron said.

A second is a long time for Cleveland sports fans, too. So much can go so wrong.

This was Game 2 of the best-of-7 Eastern Conference Finals. The Cavs had lost the opener on their home court, and they were behind 95-93 with a single second left. They had Mo Williams standing on the sideline, about 40 feet from the basket, preparing to deliver the inbounds pass.

"I told Mo, whatever — whatever it was going to take for me, I was going to come get the ball, no matter what happened," said LeBron. "If the first, third, second, if all options run, I'm going to come

get the ball and I'm going to knock down the shot."

That's the mindset of Jordan, of Bryant, of a player willing to stare failure square in the eye and not blink.

LeBron caught the ball running away from the foul line past the three-point line at the top of the key. In one wink-of-an-eye motion, he jumped and squared his shoulders to the basket in mid-air. From 25 feet away, LeBron produced a textbook jumper with only a slight fade away to create some space between the long arms of Orlando's 6-foot-10 Hedo Turkoglu. It was only for a second, but it seemed like forever, especially for Cavaliers fans who remember The Shot from Jordan knocking their team out of the playoffs in 1989. And Jordan needed all of *three* seconds.

LeBron had only a *single* second.

As the ball was in the air — spinning, rotating, rolling — just as shooting coach Chris Jent had taught LeBron, the game clock was turning to 0:00, the scoreboard screaming: ORLANDO 95, CAVALIERS 93.

If you could remember that LeBron *expected* to make that shot — even with only one second left, because LeBron insists a second is "a long time" to a star like him ...

If you could remember that LeBron *knew* he'd find a way to win the game, because after the game he admitted that he was like many kids in many drives and gyms. He played mind games with the clocking ticking down: "5-4-3-2-SHOOT-1 — BUZZ!" The ball goes in! WE WIN!

A second was long enough for LeBron to drop that rainbow of a 25-footer through the rim for three points. Only, as LeBron said after the game about Jordan and The Shot, "That guy is not in the league anymore." And the building where Jordan delivered The Shot is gone, too. It's a field in Cuyahoga Valley National Park with no clue of what happened there once upon a time.

As Cleveland fans found out, a second is such a

**THE LEBRON FILE**
LeBron won the NBA scoring title for the 2007–08 season, averaging 30 points a game. He was the first player in Cavaliers history to win it.

long, sweet time when the great player is on your side.

It was long enough for fans to come out of shock, to drive home after the game and hear the radio replay of the call by Joe Tait: "LeBron shoots ... He hit it! He Hit It!! HE HIT IT!!!" — his voice rising with each "HE HIT IT!", as if adding another point to the scoreboard to give the Cavs a victory.

It was long enough to hear Orlando star Dwight Howard mention that the final second "was like a movie" and how he'd have to watch the replay of LeBron's shot over and over again for the next few days.

"You watch classic games and you see Jordan hit game winners," said LeBron. "You go all the way back: Jerry West hitting game winners, and Magic Johnson going across the lane and hitting the jump hook against Boston. You see all these type of shots, man, always being played even when the game has left you as an individual. Hopefully I can stick my foot in that category with Magic and Jerry West and Jordan and all these other guys that made spectacular plays on the biggest stage in the world."

You may say that the Cavs eventually lost that series to Orlando, despite LeBron's version of The Shot. But remember what happened to the Bulls after Jordan's shot against the Cavs? They won the title, right?

Guess again: knocked out in the Eastern Conference Finals by Detroit. It would be two more seasons before Jordan would win his first of six NBA championships, but he has often said The Shot did set his mental stage to being ready to take on the pressure of playing for a title.

That same may happen to LeBron.

Jordan's age at the time of The Shot?

He was 26.

How about LeBron when he had the best single second in Cavs franchise history?

He was 24.

And that says LeBron has so much time on his side.

**Terry Pluto**
is a sports columnist for *The Plain Dealer*. He has twice been nominated for a Pulitzer Prize and is an eight-time winner of the Ohio Sports Writer of the Year award.

**Brian Windhorst**
is an award-winning reporter for *The Plain Dealer* and has covered the Cleveland Cavaliers since 2003. He has been a contributing writer for ESPN.com since 2006.

The authors would like to thank David Kordalski, Bill Gugliotta and *The Plain Dealer* photography staff, Susan Goldberg, Terry Egger, Roy Hewitt, Debra Adams Simmons, Shirley Stineman, Dennis Manoloff, Keith Dambrot, Jerry Colangelo, Mike D'Antoni, Craig Miller, Paul Silas, Fred McLeod, Jeff Phelps, Austin Carr, Joe Tait, Barb Wood, Patty Burdon, Beth Harmon, Jay Brophy, Mark Murphy, Jim Meyer, Geoff Beckman, Martin Smith and Pat Fernberg. Also, thanks to David Gray, Chris Andrikanich, Jane Lassar and Rob Lucas of Gray & Company.

PLAIN DEALER PHOTOGRAPH | JOHN KUNTZ, JAMES PHOTO; ALLISON CAREY, AUTHORS' PHOTO

## MVP SEASON MOMENTS

LeBron hollers with delight after slamming home an alley-oop pass in the first round of the 2009 playoffs.

PLAIN DEALER PHOTOGRAPH | TRACY BOULIAN